Go

for your life

Go

for your life

How to turn your
weekdays into weekends
through property investing

chris gray
with lowell tarling

Published in Australia by:
Go For Your Life Pty Ltd
Level 14, 309 Kent Street, Sydney, NSW 2000
PO Box N64, Grosvenor Place, NSW 1220
Phone 02 9994 8944
www.GoForYourLife.com.au

First published in Australia in 2005
Reprinted in 2006

The National Library of Australia
Cataloguing-in-Publication entry:

Gray, Chris.
Go for your life

ISBN 0-646-46318-7

1. Real estate investment - Australia. 2. Real estate
business - Australia. I. Tarling, Lowell, 1949-. II.
Title.

Designed by Allan Cornwell
Produced in China through Bookbuilder

I'd like to thank Mum and Dad for everything, and sorry for being such a pain when I was kid.

Thanks to:

Anthony Bell, Director, Bell Partners
Rod Cornish, Head of Property Research, Macquarie Bank
John Edwards, MD, Residex
Jason Field, Director, National Property Valuers NSW
Angus Raine, Director, Raine & Horne
David Rees, Head of Investment Strategy, Commonwealth Bank (CBA)
Ron Switzer, FCPA, Director Corporate Sector, CPA Australia
John Symond, MD, Aussie Home Loans
Bernard Salt, Property Partner, KPMG

The journey I have travelled is quite an emotional one and needed the support of friends. Thankyou all for your encouragement, especially Andy, Tanya and Michelle for your help with this book.

Contents

~~~~~~

Historically the foundation of great wealth has been real estate and minerals. Even with the recent 'technological revolution' real estate is the refuge for safety and security.

To quote Calvin Coolidge: 'Nothing in the world can take the place of persistence'.

I would add that in real estate, you need also to be consistent and realistic.

David Baffsky
Chairman, Accor Asia Pacific

My father taught me to work; he did not teach me to love it.
Abraham Lincoln

SECTION A
ON YOUR MARKS

chapter one

To the Reader

Why should you read this book?

Hi, my name is Chris Gray and I'm fortunate enough not to have a job. At the age of 31 I gave up being a full-time employee as I couldn't fit a 9–5 job around my busy lifestyle. It took me nine years to build the financial freedom to achieve this and by writing a book of what I have done I want to challenge you to do it in less time.

> *I believe in enjoying the very best things life can give*

I believe that property is the most stable investment that provides a decent passive return and so, hopefully, by identifying with aspects of my story you too can take the plunge into the property market. However, I have a particular way of thinking that may not suit everybody. I believe in living life to the full, every day. I believe in enjoying the very best things life can give, including material things. And I believe in borrowing money to do that.

I bought my first property at the age of 22 and the numbers that I saw did not add up. Conventional thinking of buying a one-bedroom unit, which was just about affordable, would have enslaved me for the rest of my life to pay off that mortgage. Whereas thinking differently to buy a three-bedroom house, which was not affordable according to my wages, could be almost mortgage free if I rented the two spare rooms to friends. I could see that doing conventional things would never get me away from the 9–5, it would never get me a Ferrari and it would never get me out of St Albans England and into a beachfront property in Sydney Australia. Doing things the average way will turn you into an average person. Trying something different will turn you into an exceptional performer.

> *I could see that doing conventional things would never get me away from the 9–5*

I have read many books on property and have spoken to many readers of those books. They all complain that the writer is either so super wealthy, there is no chance of them ever achieving something similar (so they may as well give up now), or they say that there is never enough detail to say exactly how they did it and how to make a start. So I'm offering you a book from someone who is wealthy but not super wealthy and I'm going to give you the detail of how I bought each property.

I have bought six properties in my life, which at the time of writing, are worth approximately $3.5 million. If the market continues to grow, as it has done historically, those properties should be worth over $50 million when I reach the age of 65, which will be a lot higher than the average superannuation nest egg. Each of the properties is unique and each one has been financed slightly differently. I have described each of the financing methods so that whether you have money or not you can identify with what I have done. I will show you that, despite what anyone says, there are no rules and you can do whatever you set out to do if you have the passion and persistence to follow it through.

At 22 I started off my investment strategy with the grand sum of $35,000 and 11 years later I own assets worth 100 times that. My $3.5 million property portfolio does have mortgages against it but the properties increase by 10% each year while the mortgages stay fixed. I'm not planning on sitting still though; each year I come up with new ideas on how to buy more property.

Liberation

I've told you a bit about me, let's take a look at where you are.

Are you significantly richer than you were a year ago or even 10 years ago?

In terms of your bank account are you significantly richer than you were a year ago or even 10 years ago? Probably not. How much have your wages gone up in the last 10 years and what have you done with that extra income if there has been a rise? Often what has happened in the past is a prediction of what will happen in the future. If you evaluate what you have done in the last 10 years and then visualise where you will be in the next 10 years, will you be happy? Often we think that by working hard all our financial dreams will come true, but do they really? I don't think so. If you want your future to be different from your past, something has to *change*.

Property can be a liberator to your life rather than a ball and chain

Just like you may spend ages dreading a bungy jump or a sky dive, but having done it you realise it wasn't that bad, the decision to buy property can be just the same. At the time, it probably all seems like such a lot of money and a burden on your finances and lifestyle. Over the following pages I will show you how property can be a liberator to your life rather than a ball and chain. I will show you how it can give you more money and freedom, how you can manage it from the other side of the world and how you can make better decisions without having to be a genius.

Don't be deceived as you read my book. It may sound as if all I want is money – but the truth is I want freedom and choice.

Does this book have all the answers? It does yes, but it depends on how you use it. This books tells my story of how I have done it and it describes how I have gone out and searched for different answers when I haven't been given the ones I want. Have you got the drive to do that too?

The majority of people who buy books never read them from cover to cover and those who do, don't take every step that they've been requested to take. The same goes for seminars – 97% of people probably end up doing very little. If reading a book 'isn't your thing' then why not try www.goforyourlife.com.au for some other ideas on how you can still achieve the ultimate lifestyle.

The only thing you need apart from this book is a dream. Something that you really want and that you can visualise every time you close your eyes. Dreams encourage successful people to carry on where others falter. Take a few minutes to really think about what you want. What if there really were no rules? What if you could have anything you wanted?

You *can* have it.

All it takes is for you to open your mind.

Summary

If you haven't turned into an overnight success in the last 10 years, what's to say that it's going to happen in the next 10 years?

Rather than aiming to buy 5–10 properties tomorrow and be super rich overnight, why not follow my more realistic plan and follow a few simple steps to buying one at a time. Property can give you a life of more freedom and less work.

Rather than blame others for where you are, take responsibility and make a change today.

ACTION PLAN

Fill in the blanks

10 years ago I was doing … and I had …

Today I am doing … and I have …

In 10 years' time I want to be doing … and I want to have …

My ultimate dream is …

Draw a picture of it and stick it on your wall.

I am committed to achieving that dream by doing …

There's nothing that can stop me from achieving my dream.

chapter two

Property Always Goes Up (in the long term)

Why should you buy property?

I have realised my dream through property; other people have done it through business or shares. The reason I prefer to do it through property is because it is solid bricks and mortar, relatively risk-free, grows 24/7 and I can manage it passively. Here are a few other thoughts why I believe it is more likely to give you the lifestyle you want compared to your other investment alternatives.

The Western economy is underpinned by property. If property collapses, so does the entire economy. The government and the Reserve Bank would not easily allow such a thing to happen. That's why property is such a stable investment and as it is so passive to look after, it is the best way of being able to afford a better lifestyle without having to work too hard.

The banks and the government want and encourage you to buy property. The banks will lend you 90%–95% and sometimes even 100% of the property value so that you only have to pay the deposit and the costs. The government then gives you a deposit in the form of a First Home Owners Grant and in some states it even reduces your costs by giving you Stamp Duty savings. Could such authoritative and established institutions like the banks and the government be offering you bad financial advice? It is not in their interest to do so.

- If the banks have lent money on virtually every property in Australia, can they afford for the property market to crash?

- If customers' $300,000 mortgages were secured by properties that had fallen from $400,000 to $200,000 then would the money markets still be investing in the banks' products?

- If all their loans were effectively worthless, would they not bring the whole economy down?

I would bet my entire portfolio – and I do – on the premise that both the left and right pillars of our society – i.e. the financial institutions and the government – would do everything in their power to protect themselves, you and the nation to keep the property market stable.

Mum and Dad Investors

I believe in having a balanced portfolio of property, shares, passive businesses and cash to give me financial stability no matter what is happening in the market. However, I do have a real passion for property as it gives me a lot of advantages over other types of investments.

It is a well-known fact that 'Mum and Dad investors' are the big losers in the sharemarket. How can they compete with professional and institutional investors who are studying pages and pages of information which are updated on their PCs every second? (Don't you think that reading the newspapers after events have happened is a bit late for that type of fluctuating investment?)

Analysing companies' financials is not easy for the person on the street. You need a high level of skill to find a share that will give you a better than average return. When the sharemarket moves up as a whole, some shares go up while others go down, whereas in the property market every house in the suburb goes up. If *every* house in your suburb is going up, how hard can it be to make a profit especially when your bank values your property to make sure that you are not overpaying?

Shares fluctuate every day and if you have borrowed money to buy them, the bank might ask for more money even if they temporarily fall in value (a 'margin call'). If your share portfolio dropped $10,000 in one day, it would hurt and you'd be feeling apprehensive. Banks don't analyse the daily prices of your home and as long as you continue to pay your mortgage they are usually very happy. Do you even notice if your property drops in value one day and rises the next?

If you polled 100 people and asked, 'Did you lose money on your residential property when you sold it?' Almost everyone – if not everyone – would say no. The main example of people losing money in property is when they have just bought it and are forced to sell it in a hurry, i.e. because of divorce or needing quick cash to get out of a financial hole.

Hold it for the long term and all losses will be turned into profits

Even in bad times property is good. Consider the late-80s when the property market crashed. If you bought at the peak and then were forced to sell a year later you might have lost money, but if you still held your property until 2005 you would have doubled, tripled or even quadrupled your money. Hold it for the long term and all losses will be turned into profits. In the long term properties never crash to zero.

I counteract the downtimes by investing for the long term

Property goes in cycles. There are bad times as well as good. I counteract the downtimes by investing for the long term because I believe that property will always go up in the end. In order to invest for the long term I need to ensure that I never have to sell in the short term. Rather than pray for it not to happen in the future, I take action now to make sure I can deal with it when it does happen.

From my perspective property has been a wonderful investment because it has given me security and stability. A lot of people who promote shares say, 'Property's not very liquid, you can't get your money out in an emergency' but generally – with being able to refinance and through lines of credit – you *can* have that liquidity in property. If you suddenly need to take money out, you don't have to sell.

I was recently asked to run a property workshop on the subject *Why Buy Property?* So I took that question to my friends to see how they'd respond and most of their reasons did not fall into any of the above categories. They didn't say things like, 'it's a wonderful investment', 'it's better than shares', 'it's bricks and mortar'. They simply wanted to own a property for personal reasons and for motives they could not necessarily explain. They said, 'I just want one'. They wanted something to live in, they wanted something to call their own, they felt that owning it would give them a comfort factor. Property is something they've been brought up to want.

> *If you haven't bought a house you'd be renting and that would be dead money*

According to David Rees, Head of Strategy Investment at CBA, 'Property breeds stability. People get into the property market because they want to live somewhere, but it turns out in the last 30–40 years that property also happens to be a good investment. It is probably the best investment available – and it can be tax free. If you haven't bought a house you'd be renting and that would be dead money – so relatively speaking you can't do much better. People eventually bought houses for that reason. It's a win-win situation because you live in it and it also turns out to be a very good investment, and that's the case throughout the Anglo-Saxon world.

Summary

Property is a solid growth investment if you can hold it for the long term. The banks and the government are reliant on the property market, and you the consumers, so they will do anything to protect you from violent shocks.

Property is very much a passive investment and you don't need to be a genius to buy it well.

ACTION PLAN

Writing down your reasons for buying property will reinforce your thoughts about why you are making a certain decision.

My reasons for investing in property are...

1.

2.

3.

chapter three

In the Red

~~~~~~

Why listen to me?

I was born in the cold and the wet of the UK and I first got my taste of a better lifestyle when I came on holiday to Australia at age 18. I loved it so much I emigrated here permanently when I was 27 and considered myself well and truly settled as an Australian when I got my passport two years later. Australia is such a good country to live in, I had more of a drive to succeed here because the less time I spent at work, the more I could spend on the beach.

In Australia you don't have to be a millionaire to live close to the CBD and right on the water. It's quality of life at a reasonable price, whereas in the UK even if you're a billionaire beachside city-living just does not exist – plus it'd be too cold to go out and enjoy it anyway.

I want to share my story with you so you can see where I'm coming from, and how I changed from being a full-time employee as an accountant to a self-confessed lifestyler. I've set up a mid-week water-ski club. The water is much flatter mid-week as, with everyone else at work, there're no other boats to disturb it and the queue for fish and chips at Watson's Bay is almost non-existent. You're welcome to come and join me – but you need to have the freedom to do so, and the steps in my book will show you how.

My father, Ken, is now a retired heart physician who worked for the Government Health Service in a hospital in North London. My mother's name is Ros and she was a nurse, until she had us kids. My sister Sarah is two years older than me, is a part-time teacher and has two kids – Daisy and Millie. My brother Tim is four years younger and works in sales for an IT security company in London.

My father was always into academia having studied Medicine at Cambridge University. He aimed for all his children to study hard and get professional jobs but I was rebellious and did the bare minimum to get by. My mum wanted me to go to an expensive private school (as it would look good for the neighbours) but my dad knew that I would waste his money and do nothing with that privileged opportunity. So I ended up going to a regular government-funded boys' school.

I didn't really enjoy school but I did enjoy bunking off and smoking behind the school theatre with the other dropouts. Even at primary school at seven years old I was very good at maths, the numbers seemed to fit together logically so I didn't have to work at it. Much to my sister's dismay, even though I spent so much time rebelling I still walked away with three A levels and nine O levels although they were only 'just passes'.

We lived in a nice house with a large garden in the country on the outskirts of London. My father was proud of the fact that he bought all his cars secondhand and saved a fortune by not buying brand new. He's happier with his 25-year-old Volkswagen than he is in something flash.

Money was never talked about in the house

Although we were a fairly well-off family, money was never talked about in the house. It wasn't taboo, but wealth wasn't a nice thing to talk about. I don't think it was just my family, I think it was the generation that my parents came from.

Go for your life

My father definitely wasn't a person to show his wealth. He would have (and still does have) holes in his clothes and would rather wear those than something brand new, and that's the way we were brought up. My parents certainly didn't see us go short, but we didn't get big handouts either. Sure, we had pocket money but we were brought up to feel that we had to earn our own money. If Sarah, Tim and I wanted to buy something special we had to earn it ourselves, which taught us the value of money. From the age of 13 I got into paper rounds and then into cleaning cars, stacking shelves in shops, delivering pizzas and even selling kitchens door to door.

However, I'm quite different to my father because I like fast cars, long holidays and all the better things in life. I've earned it, so I've got no problems spending it. I'd prefer to spend it rather than die with it all in the bank.

I finished school at 18 and rather than go to university I took a year out. I've always been into driving so when I left school my first ambition was to be some kind of racing or rally driver. My dad taught me to drive when I was about 15 and as I was too young to drive on the road, he used to let me loose in car parks and places like that. Instead of being a racing driver I had to settle for being a car courier in London. No one would give a company car to an 18-year-old so the only way to get one was to buy my own. With no money and no savings I donned a suit and dragged Dad down to the bank to help me beg for a loan. I don't know if my cheap suit or bad aftershave was the problem but the friendly bank manager didn't seem prepared to lend money to someone like me with no assets. Dad's offer of guaranteeing my $9000 loan got me over the line.

I love driving and being a car courier was one of the most enjoyable jobs I've ever had, it was very relaxed – driving around London in summer with the sunroof open and the music on. I used to deliver labels to the fashion companies in the West End. I'd be the 18-year-old spotty kid going into all these warehouses where the young female workers always took the mickey out of the delivery boy. It was really good fun having the freedom to be out and about, although by the time I bought the car and paid all my parking fines, it actually cost me.

In the Red, In Australia

Many of the kids from my village in Hertfordshire would take a year off before going to university and in that year they would usually head for Australia. I'd never been anywhere apart from Europe, yet when someone said 'Australia' I thought, 'Yep, I'll give it a go'. It was the second time I'd been on a plane.

I came to Australia for four months in 1990 and I was very poor. I lived in a backpackers' hostel on Manly Beach. I loved it even though I was working seven days a week. Just to get up and see the sun and go for a swim was the perfect kind of life for me, because no one could do that in the UK. That's what drew me to Australia – even with no money I think it's a better life here than it is anywhere else.

Because I had built up so many debts very quickly I was poor. I was $9000 in debt from buying my car after leaving school and after working for six months things were worse! – I was about $13,000 in debt from the car and going out partying. This meant that while I was overseas, I had to send money back to the UK to pay off my debts which is why I had no money for anything when I came to Australia for the first time.

I worked five days a week doing accounting for AGB Research and I also worked in a petrol station at the weekends. At this time my diet was usually a packet of biscuits for lunch (which in those days cost maybe 40c-50c) and dinner was spaghetti with tomato sauce which cost about 50c as well.

At this time I had no real interest in property and I certainly didn't have the money to buy anything even if I did have the opportunity.

The furthest I travelled in Australia was on the last weekend before leaving when I took a day trip to the Blue Mountains. I couldn't do anything like go on a scuba course and other things like that because I couldn't afford it, so I vowed that I'd do absolutely *everything* when I'd come back the next time.

And that's what I eventually did.

> *I will do whatever it takes and often I've worked double shifts or second and third jobs to get more*

I guess what drove me then and still drives me today, is that I have got aspirations to get more, and I will do whatever it takes to fulfil those aspirations. I like the 'better things' in life, that's my motivation, but I'm willing to go hard to get them. Quite often I've worked double shifts or second and third jobs to get more. I knew that I wanted to live in Australia and I discovered that accounting could get me there. When I returned to the UK I thought, 'When I did my A levels, no one cared about what O levels I got two years before. Once I go to university no one will care about my A levels and once I get my accounting qualifications no one will care what university I went to. So rather than waste four years at university being poor, why not go straight into accounting school and work at the same time?' So I went straight into work at 19 and started studying accountancy at night school in the UK.

When I was doing my accountancy studies all my friends were at university with their parents paying for them to have a good time. I knew that if I went to university my parents would barely give me enough money to survive and as they didn't like me smoking they would ensure that I didn't have too much spare money for that. Even though I hadn't had much money in my year off, the thought of having even less money for socialising as a student didn't really excite me, which is why I worked for a salary during the day. I was happy studying at night as long as I got to the pub for last orders when I finished college.

My First Massive Mortgage

The freedom of living in Australia and then returning home to live by my parents' rules was too much of a culture shock so I started to look for a place to buy. We had always been brought up to buy our homes rather than rent so renting wasn't even a consideration.

> *It could fund a lifestyle that I couldn't afford on a normal salary*

I will go into more detail later, but I found a way to buy a property that was eight times my salary as well as earn $50,000 overnight. Not only did I find that it was cheaper to buy a three-bedroom house than it was to buy a one-bedroom unit but I soon discovered that it could fund a lifestyle that I couldn't afford on a normal salary.

Second Property and Fast Cars

A lot of what differentiates me financially from other people is that I then bought a second property which took my assets and borrowings to another level. Getting used to having so much debt at a young age made me more confident with smaller finances as I knew I had bigger assets that were constantly growing. In my day-to-day life I was technically poor, mostly self-inflicted through credit cards, while on the other hand I had structured my finances in such a way that my tenants were paying off my rapidly appreciating properties. And so I allowed myself a few luxuries in life, and who can blame me for that? I'm not sure my father understood some of it, but I think he respects the results.

> *I worked out how I could buy a Porsche for virtually nothing*

My father didn't have a special interest in property, he's not a money-orientated person so I didn't really get any pushing or mentoring from him. He loves playing around with share investing, but it's more of a hobby to him than anything else.

I initially got into property to get a roof over my head but the more I got into it, and borrowing money, the more I started learning that it was an investment that could bring me other advantages. At the age of 24 I learned about refinancing from a bank advertisement and then I worked out how I could buy a Porsche for virtually nothing. So I bought one and it was one of the proudest times of my life. I can still see my cheesy grin as I drove it into my parents' drive!

African Adventure

After I finished my accountancy exams I got my visa for Australia and came up with the thought, 'I've always wanted to travel again, only this time I want to enjoy everything that I couldn't afford before!' So in 1998 I sold the Porsche which gave me a cash injection of $30,000. I took that $30,000 and said to myself, 'This is the money that I'm going to spend getting to Australia where I'll be going out and having a good time.'

The Porsche was a good learning tool too (well, this is how I justify it). Secondhand luxury sports cars don't have to cost you a lot of money but they do give a hell of a lot of pleasure! If you buy a brand new car for the same price, $30,000, you will probably lose $5000–$10,000 immediately and you will still be driving an ordinary car. Buying a secondhand Porsche for $30,000, racing it for 12 months and selling it a year later only cost me $1000 as it had already fully depreciated. Not only did it cost me $1000 for a year but I was actually driving a $100,000 car that was only a few years old.

From having a good job in the city, a Porsche, a wardrobe full of nice clothes and going out every night, I spent four months in Africa on a food budget of $1 a day, then I went to Asia for four months before travelling down the east coast of Australia until I reached Sydney. That year off was probably the happiest I've ever been, realising that I didn't actually need many material things. I *like* having all the toys and all the comforts, but I don't actually *need* them – being free, doing whatever I wanted to do, looking at the wildlife, that's the best thing, and I will certainly do more travelling when I can. It's not the wealth and the money that I really want, it's the freedom to choose what I want to do every day.

Australia II

A lot of people aren't ready to help you and give you the encouragement to move ahead. When I sat in a St Albans pub in 1998 and announced to my friends that I was heading for Australia many friends said, 'You won't hack it.' Instead of looking at the positives, they were looking at the negatives. When they heard I was going to Africa those same people said, 'You're too used to your suits and your cars, a soft person like you won't be able to backpack.' But if you're adaptable you don't need all those things, you can be happy in both situations. I wasn't bothered when they said, 'You'll fail', because at the end of the day if I couldn't hack backpacking I'd simply catch a return flight – give my tenants a month's notice to get out of my house – and I'd go back to exactly how I was before.

> *There are two types of people in life: those who encourage you and those who are scared of change*

There are two types of people in life: those who encourage you to push on and succeed, and those who are scared of change so they try to hold you back. Even though your friends want you to be a success, a lot of them are so afraid of change that they remain in the same town they've lived in all their lives. I've found that with property investing in the last 10 years, a lot of people say to me, 'It's too chancy, I wouldn't be investing…'. Or later in my story when I left my job in Deloitte's they said, 'Why would you leave a good job like that, I wouldn't be going out on my own, it's too risky, you're sure to fail.'

But there are certainly individuals who are very positive and I like being around positive people. When I'm feeling uncertain about what I'm doing – I need those good friends around me to keep pushing me and to say, 'Chris, you're doing the right thing – keep going, keep going, it'll be worth it in the end', and of course it always is. Have you experienced this too?

From a Porsche to a Ferrari

The first job I got in Australia was as an accountant at *BMCMedia.com* which quickly rose from employing 10 people to employing 100. I helped launch it on the stock exchange and the share price went from 50 cents up to $7.50 in a surprisingly short time.

There were many great things about this enterprise, such as the owners giving everyone a part of the company in the form of share options. Our MD wanted to help all the young 20-year-olds turn their options into deposits for their first homes. If he managed to turn 5000 options into $10,000–$20,000 that an employee could use as a deposit on a property, he was a happy man. That's one of the most generous gestures I've seen in business – to give your staff a start in life.

He was a smart guy – not only did he have good intentions, he also came up with concepts that would really make me think. He said, 'When you're wealthy – say you have $10 million – your lifestyle doesn't change if you earn another $10 million. You don't have twice as many cars or twice as big a house. You just give more to charity.'

> *If you work all your life and then you die, what's the point?*

From him I learned that money isn't an end in itself. It's there to be enjoyed, because if you work all your life and then you die, what's the point?

Not only did the MD give me good advice, but one of the venture capitalists did too. He said, 'Greed will make you go bust. You've got to take your profits when you can. If the market changes for the worst, there's nothing you can do about it, no matter how good the company is the shares will go down.'

> *I bet a year's salary on the stock exchange*

As well as being given options, I bet a year's salary on the stock exchange when they floated the company. Within four days my shares went from 50 cents to $1.25. Even though I was keen to double my money again, I remembered what the venture capitalist had told me. My $50,000 had turned into $125,000, so I bought my first Ferrari.

This dotcom company was so puffed full of energy it was unbelievable. We were all working 14–16 hours a day. If I wanted to meet a friend after work, my immediate boss would say, 'Get back to your desk, you've got to keep working.'

I could never finish all my work, no one could. It was never-ending. There was always pressure to work on the weekend and I thought, 'No matter how much money you pay me, it's just not worth it.'

I should have seen this coming at the outset because at the end of my first week my boss said, 'Are you coming in over the weekend?'

I said, 'No way, I'm off to the beach.'

Learning to Sell

I left the dotcom business and joined *Robert Half International* where I worked for the next nine months. It was a recruiting firm trying to place accountants into organisations either on a part-time basis or as permanent staff.

This was where I learned how to sell.

I didn't want to be a full-time salesperson but I did want to learn the communication skills in which they are rigorously trained. Accountants only get technical training and are often bad communicators, whereas through this experience I learned how to how to talk to people, how to organise meetings and how to negotiate. Because of the state of the market the majority of the job turned out to be selling and cold calling.

In fact, all I did was sell!

Deloitte's

Next I moved to the big accounting firm Deloitte Touche Tohmatsu where my job was to interview finance directors, financial controllers and accountants and coach them to get them back into the workforce or into better jobs than they were currently in.

From my exposure to recruiting I discovered that the general job market is so ageist that once you're over 45, if you get pulled out of a job at the wrong time it can wipe you out. I could see that my initial idea of being an accountant as a 'job for life' was certainly no job for life.

I saw well-educated 50–60-year-olds scrabbling around for work and settling for the same $30–40 per hour wages as 22–25 year-old backpackers with no experience. There were 60-year-olds complaining that their superannuation and life savings had suddenly been halved by the sharemarket, which is the reason they had to carry on working! Seeing things like that teaches you lots of lessons – but it's better to learn them at 30 rather than at 60 when it's getting too late.

The 9–5 didn't seem to make sense to me any more

Straight away I thought to myself, 'I'm never going to be as clever as those CEOs and if that's what's life's going to be like at 50, what's the point in spending the next 20 years climbing the ladder with all the other corporate sheep?'

In 2002, at age 31, I was working 40 hours a week and earning about $50,000–$60,000 after tax. At the same time I had five properties that were growing in excess of $50,000–$60,000 per year each without me spending any time on them. The 9–5 didn't seem to make sense to me any more.

Summary

I was a fairly average person with a good upbringing but I decided early on that I didn't want to have an average lifestyle. Australia is a great place no matter how much money you do or don't have. I didn't want to waste my life by being stuck in an office.

I found a way to buy a property that was eight times my salary as well as earn $50,000 overnight. I then found a way to buy a second, third…sixth property and now have a portfolio worth about $3.5million.

Giving up a full-time job at the age of 31 was the best thing I ever did and I recommend everyone else should give it a go if they have the dreams and aspirations to have more.

ACTION PLAN

These are the things that motivate me in my life …

This is what's missing from my life …

This is what I am prepared to do to achieve those ends…

chapter four

Step One: Set Your Goals

You need to set goals to achieve your dreams

Rather than trusting to luck, I believe you should plan all your property moves. The first step that most people take is to go out on a Saturday morning and look at property. How can you choose between different types of properties when you haven't built a plan of what you're trying to achieve? Looking at property is more exciting than sitting down with pen and paper, but if you're short of time and are looking at achieving your goals in the most efficient time frame, having a set of written goals is definitely the most important first step.

'I don't know much about it, but I know what I like,' is an old adage which most people subscribe to when buying property – they simply know what they like. There is no other category of investment in which people can operate like that. And they get away with it for two reasons. Firstly, because over the past decade it has been difficult to make a mistake because virtually every property has appreciated, sometimes hugely. And secondly, because they like it and therefore they live in it. By the time the dream is over, they've probably doubled their money. And so the cycle starts again.

Goal-setting is about establishing what you want to achieve, breaking it down into lots of steps and doing just one thing a week. I had a life coach who, amongst other things, helped me overcome the mental fear of leaving the security of a full-time job. One of the most important things she taught me about goal-setting was to break things down. So when it comes down to buying your first property I have designed a course which breaks the steps into six weeks and I ask people to do one little thing a week, then suddenly it's not such a big deal.

Me-time

Wealth to me isn't about money – it's about choice

Wealth to me isn't about money – it's about choice. One million dollars in the bank isn't going to make you happy, the happiness lies in the choices that $1 million can give.

Unless your dream is really strong you'll still be in the same position

Unless your dream is really strong, the years will pass you by and you'll still be in the same position, but a *burning desire* will drive you.

Most people never take the time to think about their own challenges, and that's how having a life coach really helped me. When I had a day-job, no matter how busy I was my coaching session would force me to think about *me* for an hour a week. My coach documented every session so there was no going back on my word. (You can think it through in your mind, but until you put it down on paper, it isn't really real. You've definitely got to write it down. Every day I come up with ideas which I write in my diary so that I don't forget to act on them, that's my way of doing it.)

I like the Smart Goals system. Over the years lots of people have told me about it, I tracked it through the Internet and after applying it to my own situation, I put my own slant on it to suit my personal growth needs. When applied to goal-setting, SMART stands for:

- S – specific
- M – measurable
- A – achievable
- R – realistic
- T – time driven

Specific

S is for specific. Your goal has got to be specific because if it's not specific you can claim anything you like. For example you could say, 'I want to retire rich.' Now 'rich' has got no specific meaning and if you don't achieve much you can make excuses like, 'Actually $100,000 to me is rich' rather than the $1 million you were thinking before. But if you work it out and write something specific, like 'I need $1 million to do all the things that I want to do when I retire', there are two advantages – (1) you can't fool yourself, plus (2) you keep reminding yourself.

Remind yourself every day that you will achieve your over-riding goal. For example, a lot of people will have their 'goal words' facing them on their desk. Some people position them on the shaving mirror, where they brush their teeth, on their coffee mug or somewhere like that.

They do it because for those 2–3 minutes per day they can see their goal of 'I don't want to work for the rest of my life' staring them in the eye. This should give them the motivation to make the extra effort because they will be reminded that doing so contributes directly to their ultimate success. I know someone who even hangs her goal in a picture frame. Another person, someone who wants to sail the world, has a picture of the yacht right up there on his wall. Every time he lifts his eyes from his computer, that's what he sees. As for me, of course, I keep written goals, but I also display photographs of my African trip around my walls to remind me of one of the happiest experiences of my life, and to encourage me to work hard to get back there again.

So write your specific goal and display it. Some days I'm sure you wake up a bit grumpy or a bit hung over and you don't want to go to work. But then you'll see the picture of the blue ocean and the blue skies – that will hopefully give you that extra bit of drive to say, 'I'm going to work today because – incrementally – it will help me achieve my dream!'

Measurable

M is for measurable – you've got to have numbers in your written goal so that you can break it into bite-sized chunks. Putting figures to your goals will enable you to break them into the smallest equations.

If you want to get $1 million by the time you're 65 you might say:

- 'I'll need to purchase five properties to achieve that.'
- 'To get those five properties I'll need to save $50,000 as a deposit to get the ball rolling.'
- 'To get that $50,000 I'll need to save maybe $2000–$3000 a month for a certain period of time.'
- 'And to do that I'll need to achieve a bonus within my current job to give me $2000 a month to give me the extra money to save.'
- 'If I want an extra $2000 I'll have to sell a certain amount of product.'
- 'To sell that amount I've got to have 10 meetings with clients because every 10 meetings I have with clients, leads to me getting one more sale.'
- 'To get 10 meetings I'll have to speak to 30 people.'
- 'To speak to 30 people I've got to ring 50.'
- 'Therefore my goal is: I've got to ring 50 new customers a week, which means I've got to ring 10 each day.'

> *The ultimate goal of $1 million must be constantly broken down into smaller regular activities*

In this way the ultimate goal of $1 million must be constantly broken down-and-down-and-down, into smaller regular activities such as phone calls, in this example. A baker can break it into bags of flour, a manufacturer into units.

From one week to the next you won't be able to feel whether or not you're nearer to your $1 million but you will always be able to know very specifically whether you've rung your 10 clients.

It's very difficult to accumulate $1 million in assets – but it's very easy to ring 10 customers today. And it's easy because it's measurable. You can trust those figures.

Achievable

A is for achievable – because it can't be 'out of reach', it's got to be something you can potentially get or do:

- To ring 50 customers in a week is a lot of customers.
- To ring 10 a day is not too bad.
- If you break it down to five in the morning and five in the afternoon that's even easier.

> *Try to think of a way to make it fun*

It doesn't have to be difficult. Try to think of a way to make it fun. This is one of the other things my life coach taught me – there is no logical reason to say 'don't take the easy option'. If there's an easy option – take it!

For example, you could say, 'I'm booking time out of my diary, I'm walking away from the noise and the hassle of the office, I'm going to sit in the park and I'm not going to come back until I've rung 5–10 people.' So make it enjoyable and then you'll actually look forward to making those calls because you will be working in the fresh air.

Realistic

R is for realistic which builds on 'achievable'.

Don't set too many goals. If you over-reach you'll find yourself constantly coming up with failure. Better for morale and for the bank balance to have lots of little wins rather than one big hit/miss gamble. Over-reaching doesn't pay. Set one or two goals and concentrate in those areas. Think long-term – realise now that the more you achieve, the more you can take on further down the line.

Time-driven

T – there's got to be a time-line.

The ultimate dream is to have the lifestyle you want. An example of a time-line is, 'At the age of 65 I want to be able to retire on $1 million worth of assets.' To build up to that goal you've got to break that down to – say – 'I've got to buy five properties to get to the $1 million and I've got to do one now, one in five years time, one in 10 years, one in 15 years…'. I always bring it back to financials because I'm an accountant.

The timeframe makes you *start* rather than talk about it. If you wait until tomorrow your energy will only be half as much, and the day after half as much again – and the Law of Diminishing Returns suggests to me that you'll never do it unless you start now. You've got the energy to do it *now* because you're thinking about it *now*. No matter what you want to do – the time to do it is always *now*.

Small Rewards

As you travel along your goal program I suggest you give yourself small rewards – so if you ring your 10 people you say, 'Each time I achieve my

10 calls I can go out and get a latté.' I really believe in celebration. If you receive a benefit, that pushes you on. I think that's really important.

Create a situation where you can make yourself believe that all the time spent working is giving you some immediate benefit as well. If you've agreed to save $500 per month, try to give yourself some kind of reward too, so you don't just think of your goal-setting program as take-take-take all the time. To get the reward sometimes requires pushing yourself harder and saying, 'I'll earn $700 but out of that $700 I'll spend $200 on myself and still save my $500. I'll book into a 5-star hotel, go for a massage and really pamper myself. I'll go to a show! I'll do something like that!'

I've always been very good at that, but often I reward myself before I actually achieve those goals.

You've got to do the hard work as well.

Sacrifice

Sometimes you've got to make a sacrifice

Sometimes you've got to make a sacrifice to achieve your goal and that makes it even more worthwhile when you to achieve success.

I've sacrificed a lot of free time in the evenings and weekends to read books, go on courses and run around looking at properties. It wasn't all rosy at the time, but nine years of hard work was worth it to create 35 years of not having to work.

Make a sacrifice and it will come back to you 10-fold.

Publicise Your Commitment to Your Goal

Having a private goal hidden away in your diary is all well and good but if you fail to achieve it no one will ever know. Telling your family, friends, colleagues and the rest of the world will get it out in the open, so that each time you think of giving up, you will be reminded of your commitment.

Summary

Physically setting and writing down your goals significantly increases the chances of you actually achieving them. Display them prominently, read them every day and act on them – and you'll be unstoppable.

Make your goals specific, measurable, achievable, realistic and time-driven to ensure that they are real goals.

ACTION PLAN

My 10-year goal is to...

My 3-year goal is to ...

My 1-year goal is to ...

I am committed to do the following in the next four weeks ...

and I will start today.

chapter five

Get Rid of Your Job

Why you should focus less on your job

I never wanted to work hard for a living. Why would I aspire to be in a workplace where I didn't want to be when the alternative was to go out and have fun?

I think a lot of people have been brought up to believe that you've got to work hard to hold your head high and say to your family, 'I'm the breadwinner, I do a hard day's work and I deserve your respect...!'

Throughout my upbringing there seemed to be this big thing in society that you've got to 'work hard' but – honestly – I think deep down a lot of people aspire to *not* have to work. They don't want to work but they don't want a drop in income. They want both, and they could strive to have both but because they won't get out of their comfort zone they're happy to kid themselves and their listeners by saying, 'I really enjoy my job and that's what I want to do for the rest of my life.' Even though a minority of people really do enjoy their jobs, especially when they're community-related, I think most other people would not continue in their jobs if they had the money. They only go to work because they can't afford not to. The flip side of that is when they spend their whole lives working so hard they don't have any other interests. Then they can't give up work because it is all they know. On your gravestone do you really want to see the words, *All s/he did was work*?

> *Rather than have one job and one property, why not have no job and two properties?*

One of the things that influenced my thinking was that many of my friends' parents were well-paid professionals. Even though they had healthy salaries and pensions I would suggest that a lot of their retirement wealth was generated by the increased value of their properties over the last 40 years of their working lives. Throughout my childhood I noted that most people had one property and one job. I did the maths on that and I remember thinking, 'I'll never be as clever or as well paid as them so rather than have one job and one property, why not have no job and two properties? And if I can have no job and two properties why not have three, four or five properties. Hell, why not have 20 or 30?'

> *Did you earn more than your property today?*

Many years later I saw an advertisement on television from one of the banks which confirmed this idea. It showed a person leaving the house and going to work in the early morning darkness and then returning in the dark of night. The caption then said, 'Did you earn more than your property today?'

When I was interviewing finance directors and dealing with people's wages I realised that just because people had high salaries, it did not necessarily mean that they had money to burn. The more people earned, the more they had to work and the less time they had to enjoy their lifestyle.

You Can't Save What Your Property Can Earn

Working for a living wasn't the most logical way for me to achieve my financial goals and it certainly wouldn't be bringing me happiness and wealth.

In London a lot of my male friends were in the banking sector. Believe it or not they used to challenge each other to see who did the most hours in the week. They'd take the attitude, 'I'm the man, I worked 18 hours yesterday!' My flatmate took it to the extreme of only going home when he actually fell off his chair from exhaustion. Whereas I'd always prefer to say, 'I did all of my work yesterday in two hours, and I spent the rest of the day in the sunshine.'

To earn $100,000–$150,000+ per annum in Australia you've generally got to work from 7.00am until 7.00 at night five, six, seven days a week – what's the point?

A lot of people think a pay rise or a bonus is the answer

A lot of people think a pay rise or a bonus is the answer. However, if you get a $20,000 pay rise, that's only $10,000 after tax which is an increase of less than $1000 a month – and an extra $1000 a month isn't going to really change your lifestyle and it certainly isn't going to make you rich! All it will do is allow you to eat slightly better meals, wear slightly better clothes, drive a slightly better car – once you've done those three things you'll find that your $1000 per month has suddenly disappeared. How often can you expect a $20,000 pay rise?

If you take a look around your immediate circle of friends or parents' friends you will note how much their properties have gone up. Compare that figure with how much you can potentially save from working – it's no contest. For example if you bought a property for $400,000 and over 3–4 years it went up 25% to $500,000, that would be an annual saving of $25,000 per year. A 25% rise is a conservative rise but how many people do you know who save $25,000 every year from their wages? Not many.

I am also trying to put forward the idea that most of our parents have made a lot of money from property in the last 20–30 years and if they had concentrated on buying even one additional property rather than solely trying to pay off their mortgage they would now be in a much better financial position.

Not the Golden Child

While I've done a lot of sensible things in terms of buying property I'm certainly not the golden child who does everything perfectly. I could have been a lot further ahead if I had controlled my personal spending. I've spent a lot of money, it's true, but I've always had assets behind me to balance that and I've had a professional income to balance that as well.

I know that if I didn't spend so much money, I could be a lot further ahead than where I am now, but I really believe in enjoying life. I'd rather reach 50% of my potential and have a wonderful life than reach 100% of my potential through working 50–60 hours a week for 50 years.

If I had enough money in the bank to sit on my boat, race cars, look at the sea, enjoy nature, to be honest, I'd be pretty happy doing that – which is what I did for a year after leaving Deloitte's. I found that I was busier without a job than when I had one. I was as happy as I was in Africa when I had a limited income but an unlimited lifestyle.

Investing in property creates enormous passive wealth

Investing in property creates enormous passive wealth which will make you asset rich to pay for all the expensive things in life. However you still need an income to finance those properties and to live day-to-day. Whilst the rent will pay a high proportion of this, you will often need an additional source of income. But as you are creating this big asset base you can be less reliant on having a career. At Deloitte's my friends and colleagues kept asking for my advice in property investing and as I enjoy teaching I coached them for free. I have now turned this into my part-time business which creates enough income to support me day-to-day. No matter how much I charge per hour I will never get rich as I am limited by the hours in the day. It's only by adding to my property portfolio that I really become wealthier as there is no real limit to how much I can buy and the properties work 24/7. That is what gives me more choice in the future.

I like being in corporate life, but I don't want to go back to it full-time. I am building a business that will educate people in property investing to help them build a better lifestyle away from work. There are lots of other things I thought about doing instead: I could be an accountant, an investment consultant or I could work in executive recruitment; but when I wrote a list of what I enjoy doing most, top of the list was educating people about property. I love property and I love educating people because there's nothing more rewarding than seeing the change in the people I have taught.

What if one of us lost our job?

A couple I coach are on reasonable salaries – they had the deposit for a property but they couldn't bring themselves to buy anything because they were worried about having a big mortgage, starting a family and 'what if one of us lost our job?' I sat down with them and helped bring some reality to the issues they thought they were facing. Many of these issues were just preconceptions and ended up not being real problems at all. Eventually they bought a unit and they bought really well. The whole experience completely changed their lives, they are currently on a plan to build a property portfolio for the rest of their lives and to spend less time at work.

Their property rose in value and within a few months they had $50,000 equity. The baby came and the wife stopped working for three months. Since they'd made $50,000 she felt more secure not working and felt she could afford to spend more time with the baby. Instead of panicking, 'We've only got one salary!' they rented out the unit and urged me to help them buy another one because they wanted to make even more money. And then – after the wife had done her three months at home – he took two months off to spend time with their child.

Their lives have now improved for the better and they are building a plan to spend less time at work and more with their young family. I only did a tiny little thing – they were literally on the edge of buying and I managed to push them over the other side. Having that kind of experience gives me enormous satisfaction.

Money Gives You Choices

In my first role as an accountant in Sydney Australia I worked for *BMCMedia.com* which was listing on the stock market. As it got closer to the launch the working days got longer and my evenings and weekends got shorter. Even after the launch the hours seemed to continue. I left after one year. No matter how much I was paid, I could not justify missing out on enjoying myself in my late 20s, when I should be out socialising and enjoying the fresh air at the beach.

I believe in working hard for an employer but I disagree with them putting pressure on you to put in excess hours. Some employers such as Deloitte's were great: you were judged on what you produced and not what hours you clocked in. What is your employer like?

I would rarely give up my evenings and weekends for an employer but when you choose what you want to do for a living there is no difference between a weekday or a weekend; they each hold equal possibilities. Money allows me the freedom to choose the balance myself.

If I need to kip on the Monday afternoon – I do

The other Friday I took my girlfriend out on Sydney Harbour, then we took the boat to the Fish Markets for lunch. There was not a soul on the harbour, we had all that peace and quiet to ourselves. We both chose to work on the Saturday which didn't matter as we had had such a wonderful time the day before. Although I wouldn't be keen to do it for an employer, I often get up at 6.00am to go to a networking group and I often attend business functions until 10.00–11.00 at night. Working late doesn't matter because it's my choice and I can take the next day off if necessary. If I need to kip on the Monday afternoon – I do. Would your employer allow you to do that? It's true that money doesn't make you happy but it does give you more freedom and choice in how you run your life. Wealth is about having the choice. And choice to me is the fruit of wealth – even if you're driving around in an old banger, you're a wealthy person so long as you've got that choice.

Why Would I Want an Office?

I've been looking to set up some joint ventures and it surprises me that when people get interested one of the first things they say is, 'Let's get an office in the city' to which I reply, 'Why would I want an office? My place overlooks the sea – why shouldn't I work there?' I don't have to be in an office, my mobile phone is all I need to run my business. I can hold a meeting on the boat, in the car – in fact I recently did a television interview driving around in the Ferrari.

I enjoy the pin-stripe suit but I also like doing the shorts and T-shirt thing. I want to bring up a family that has a father who is not in the office from dawn till dusk.

> *Traditional business implies you've got to have an office*

Traditional business implies you've got to have an office, but in reality – largely because of technology – that is no longer true. Some people spend an hour commuting to work whereas – because I avoid all rush hours – it only takes me 10 minutes to get into the city. Sometimes I work at my desk in my dressing gown; meanwhile, my flatmate Barry White (from Essex – not the singer), who wakes up around the same time, gets to his desk an hour and a half later because he's got to shave, put on a suit, catch a bus and all the rest of it. Just like I'm working right now as I'm writing this book, I'm wearing jeans and a T-shirt and every couple of hours I wander around in the St Ives bush to take a break. This is no less 'work' than what people do in an office.

A friend of mine had a business in Queensland where the company bought a mansion for all the staff to work in as an alternative to going to an office. None of the people live there but each day they turn up to work where they have a pool, lovely views and other comforts. All in all it's an ideal place to work.

This friend thought about doing a similar thing in Sydney; he said, 'Why don't we share a penthouse in the city and that'll be our office?'

I said, 'Well, even though that would be great, I still don't want to turn up to an office and do the regular 9–5 thing and get stuck in rush hour. Why not get a boat and do our business from there? For a similar price to renting an office you can surely rent or buy a boat? Would our clients and suppliers not feel happier in a more relaxed environment? It would certainly make doing business with us a more pleasurable experience. That conversation hasn't progressed since, and I'm not sure how practical it is but it certainly sounds more fun doesn't it?

Anything you can do to make work more enjoyable will mean you will want to do more of it. Keep thinking up ideas to have a better life.

Summary

Just because your parents have been brought up to have a job for life it doesn't mean that you have to do the same. Every successful entrepreneur broke rules when others said they shouldn't, so why don't you?

Property continues to grow 24/7

Property continues to grow 24/7 whereas your work-output is limited by the number of available hours in your day. No matter what you charge per hour, can you save the same amount of money that a few properties can grow each and every year?

Rather than have one job and one property, why not have no job and two properties? If you carry on doing what you do year after year, will you ever reach your ultimate goals?

If you had $5 million in the bank would you still continue your 40–50 hour week? Go on, dream a bit!

ACTION PLAN

What I enjoy about my job is …

What I dislike about my job is …

My job is helping me achieve my ultimate goal because …

My job is stopping me from achieving my ultimate goal because …

I am going to make the following changes to help me achieve my ultimate goal …

chapter six

Step Two: What You Own and What You Owe (figure it out)

Understanding the numbers will help you invest

At the start of this book I said you need a dream to be successful and that's still true. You need to play with some numbers to make sure that your dream is realistic and can come true. You might hate numbers and I can understand that most people don't find them too exciting and that's why I became a reformed accountant rather than a practising one!

> *Imagine never having to think about whether you can afford it or not*

Sorting out the little things now will allow you to build investments so that you never have to go through the whole process again. Imagine getting invitations to go out for dinner or to go on holiday and never having to think about whether you can afford it or not. It's a wonderful feeling but you'll need to do the hard yards first. The sooner you do it the better.

Sometimes we live in a dream world and then the bills and the bank statements come through the mail and they paint another picture. If you are going to invest in property you really need to get your finances in order, otherwise no one is going to lend you money. Even if you hate the word 'budget' it is imperative to get an accurate picture of how much money is coming in each month and what is going out. I'm not here to lecture you about spending less because having never really spent less myself, I wouldn't be able to give such advice with any conviction. At least if you're going to spend up, know how much you have got to spend without getting into too much trouble. If you've already got a deposit or some equity for your next purchase then this is maybe not so important, but if you're short of both then now is the time to fix things and start a savings plan.

> *You've got to change something otherwise everything will remain the same*

Just remember – what you have done in the last 10 years is an indication of what you will do in the next 10 years. If you're not wealthy now, rather than question why I am asking you to take action – be different – for once, 'just do it'. This is just as true if you want to get into shares, property or any other form of investment, but you've got to change something – otherwise everything will remain the same. If you don't know where to start, try an Internet search and type in the words 'personal budget' and 'money saving tips'. Try out a few of the free sites. The banks and mortgage companies also have good calculators on their sites which are really easy to use.

> *If you could save 10% across-the-board on everything that you spend, that would certainly add up to a significant sum*

You can have a lot of sleepless nights if you're worried about bills coming through your door. If you could save 10% across-the-board on everything that you spend, that would certainly add up to a significant sum, which you could potentially use for property investments. Say you earn $3000–$5000 per month all of which you habitually spend each month; if you found a way to shave 10% off everything, you'd be left with $300–$500 to save/invest which is another $3600–$6000 a year. However, we often spend more than our income and so we accumulate credit card debts which only magnifies the problems.

Money savers

Here are few ideas to save a little bit more so that you can invest a little bit more:

- **Set up a savings account**

  Set up a savings account and commit yourself to saving a certain amount of money per month. Set up an automatic standing order so it gets transferred after your wages get paid in.

- **Get a longer term deposit account**

  Get a longer term deposit account that you can't access on impulse because it requires a week or a month's notice to draw the money out. A little thing like that will stop you from jumping into it at every whim.

- **Use public transport**

  If you drive to work every day you will be paying car park charges, petrol, fines, wear and tear on the car and all the rest of it. Maybe once or twice a week you could catch the bus instead, effectively saving 10% of your car-related expenditure. You might even enjoy public transport and just think of that extra time you will generate for book reading or studying the property pages. It may even be worth doing it every day? Potentially worth $300+/mth.

- **Bring a cut lunch**

  If you usually go out for a quick lunch every day it probably costs you $5–$10 to get a feed, why not make your own sandwich and carry it to work in your bag? It's not going to really affect your life, unless you are a terrible cook – and you don't have to be a cordon bleu chef to make a sandwich. Potentially worth $200+/mth.

- **Less eating out**

  If you go out for dinner once a week, try going out once a fortnight instead. Potentially worth $100+/mth even at the cheapest restaurant.

- **Buy cheaper wine**

  Buy cheaper wine. Can you honestly tell the difference between the $15 and $25 wine? Potentially worth $50+/mth.

- **Spend less on your groceries**

  There are lots of shopping tricks – buy the 'specials', shop around, buy Home Brand goods. Do a taste test at home with your family – see if they can tell the difference between the generic branded milk and butter? In some instances we know it's exactly the same product. Potentially worth $100+/mth.

- **Cut back (or cut up) your credit cards**

  Reduce your number of credit cards, you only really need one. Saving the $100 membership fee on 3–4 cards is quite a bit of money. Cutting up your cards will definitely save you $thousands!

- **Stop buying newspapers and magazines**

  Instead of spending money on newspapers and magazines, read them at work if your office pays for them. They are also available free at all public libraries and in many fast food outlets. Potentially worth $50–$100+/mth.

- **Sleep on purchases over $100 for at least 24 hours**

  How many tools, gadgets and playthings have you got that you've only used once? Delaying a major purchase for 24 hours normally brings the realisation that you don't really need it.

I could make a long list of money-savers, but as this isn't a consumer handbook, I won't. There are ways to download free music instead of buying CDs, all perfectly legal. There are ways to cut down on DVD hire, like watching them with friends. There are ways to spend less on clothes (call on the rag trade end of town instead of department stores!). Saving money is easier than you think. All it takes is discipline.

Just as there are quite a few strategies for reducing your liabilities you can possibly find ways to increase your income as well, like working overtime, putting in an extra hour a day, running a regular garage sale, or whatever you can think of. Perhaps you could work an evening job. Maybe you could negotiate a payrise or something like that – but once you've actually set up those strategies, you've got to commit that money to investing in your long-term goal.

What's In and What's Out

Now you've seen what's coming in and out in the future you need to see what you have got to work with, which is where we come to assets (good) and liabilities (bad). You need to understand these in basic detail as the two of them together make up your wealth.

An asset is defined as being 'something that has a monetary value' or in street talk, 'something that puts money in your pocket'. There are good and bad sides to some of these assets – if you get away from the dictionary definition. The opposite to an asset is a 'liability' and therefore 'something that takes money out of your pocket'.

For example, a car is both an asset and a liability. It's an asset because you can sell it, but at the same time it's a liability because you've got to keep paying for it. Even when you've paid off your car, it's still somewhat of a liability because you're still paying insurance, maintenance and running costs.

Some people say your house is not actually an asset, it's a liability because it takes money out of your pocket when you pay the maintenance, services, mortgage and everything else. But because it's actually going up in value and you can sell it, I believe that it is one of the best assets you can have.

Balance Sheet

A balance sheet is a list of all your assets and liabilities. The 'bottom line' is the difference between the two. For example, you might have a house that's worth $400,000 and you might have a mortgage of – say – $200,000 – so your net assets would be $400,000 less $200,000, which equals $200,000.

Balance Sheet

Assets (house)	$400,000
Liabilities (mortgage)	– $200,000
Net Assets (equity)	$200,000

Paradoxically, even though property costs you money you can sell it, so it's an asset.

Statement of Position

For your own personal statement of position you should write up all the things of value you've got, but when it comes to getting a mortgage, the banks are mainly interested only in property assets.

Antiques and collectibles are assets but not usable for mortgage purposes unless you sell them and use the money as a deposit. If you really needed to borrow money you could go to an art dealer who specialises in lending money against art. If you gave possession of the painting, you would probably get the loan.

Collectible assets, like rare guitars, art and stamp collections are of less interest to the bank because their portability means that you can effectively sell them off straight away, and this is why they cannot be listed as collateral in the same way as property which you can't sell overnight without the bank knowing. That's why such assets don't really add up to much when banks are calculating how much money they will lend you. They also have no interest in selling off secondhand assets.

Furthermore, the banks know that there is a changeable market for paintings, antiques and collectibles. Your art piece might fall out of fashion whereas property can be counted on to steadily appreciate. The price of a property doesn't radically change from day to day whereas the price of a painting could fall from $100,000 to $50,000 in one month. Furthermore, collectible assets can be destroyed – burned! – whereas land value is sometimes more valuable than the building, and the land always remains.

Banks will certainly credit artworks and collectibles to your balance sheet, but they won't look at lending money against them because in the event of you going bad, they may not be able to grab these things. You may have already sold them. But a house is immovable, and you can't sell it without the bank knowing because they're holding the mortgage papers and can repossess the house. Because there are so many people buying and selling real estate, as far as the bank is concerned it's a very straightforward market and if you don't pay your mortgage the lender can easily sell your property on the open market.

Assets

- **Property** is an asset.
- A **bank account** is an asset (unless it's overdrawn).
- **Shares** are assets.
- **Insurance policies** are sometimes an asset (but if you don't get the payout until you die it's of little value).
- A bank may look at lending money against certain **business equipment**. They may lend money against a big item like a $100,000 fridge or something like that, because it can readily be resold if you forfeit.

- The ownership of certain **licences** (cab, mining, professional fishing licence, etc.) are assets and you can potentially borrow against them. But you may have to go to the commercial section of the bank where you will be assigned to someone who understands their significance. The lender may charge a higher interest rate and more up-front fees to run such a loan, because to them it's a higher risk than property.

- I never include **furniture** in my personal balance sheet because it diminishes in value on a daily basis. And I'm never going to sell it because I always need a table to work on, a bed to sleep in and a couch to sit on. Listing them on my balance sheet doesn't really do me any good.

Liabilities

- Mortgages are liabilities as they are monies the bank lent you to buy a property.

- Share loan accounts/or margin lending accounts are liabilities as they relate to money borrowed to buy shares.

- Personal loans are all liabilities no matter what you used the money for.

- Any money owing on a credit card is a liability.

A balance sheet or your 'net assets' is the difference between all of your assets and liabilities.

So if you've got net assets that are positive, say $100,000, then that's good news because that means if you sold everything, paid your debts, you'd be left with $100,000. Whereas if you've got net assets of minus $100,000 (credit card debts, bank loans…) that's bad news because it means if you sold everything you'd still owe $100,000.

Balance Sheet	Good	Bad
House	$400,000	$400,000
Mortgage	-$300,000	-$350,000
Loans and Credit cards	$0	-$150,000
Net Assets (equity)	$100,000	-$100,000

Net assets create wealth and wealth creates choices. Ideally you always want to have net assets and you want to keep building them for the future.

Understanding these assets and liabilities is really important if you want to move on as an investor. I became an accountant so I could understand these types of finances but I knew that I only needed to understand the basics and not the minute intricacies.

Summary

You generally need a deposit to buy property so if you haven't got lots saved already and you haven't got parents or friends to help you out then it's time to save some money yourself.

Getting wealthier is all about having more money. You've got to understand what money you've got coming in and out if you are to understand how to get more of it. Concentrate on where it can get you and just get on with the task in hand.

It's confronting and scary but just think of the pleasure when you never have to deal with it again.

ACTION PLAN

This is what comes in and out each month

Income

Expenditure

This is what I am prepared to cut back on

This is what I am prepared to save

I will set up a savings account if I have not already got one

These are my assets

These are my liabilities

This is what I am worth

chapter seven

Protect Your Credit File

Why you would want to protect your credit

I f you want to buy property then you'll probably want to borrow some money. And when you ask to borrow money, lenders check your credit file. It's like your driving record except it's a list of all your official financial records. Just as a bad driving record will hinder you from getting insurance and cost you more, a bad credit file will hinder you from borrowing money and also costs you a higher interest rate.

> *A bad credit file will hinder you from borrowing money and also costs you a higher interest rate*

It is worthwhile keeping your credit file in first class shape, cleaning out wrong information, and, if you can, getting rid of the things that don't look good. Be careful to whom you grant access to your credit file and minimise the number of people who can access it.

Your credit file comprises not only the history of all the loans you've taken out but also all the times you've applied for loans. For example, if you apply for a mortgage at 10 different banks, that's 10 'hits' on your credit file.

That might indicate to some lenders that either you're being turned down or that you're trying to get 10 loans at the same time, which would make them extremely nervous. Certainly shop around for the best deal but don't complete the final application or the permission to check your credit file until you've decided that's the specific loan you want. Never do it on spec. Big brother is watching you.

Banks handle so many transactions that they make them as automated as possible. When going for a loan you've got to remember you're being scrutinised by a computer system, not by a human. You may write in your application that 'I'm checking out 10 different banks' but the computer won't understand that you're shopping around, so it'll just assume the worst. Computers are unimaginative like that.

Black Books

I always make sure my mortgages get paid first

I always make sure my mortgages get paid first. If you don't pay your mortgage the bank can throw you out of your house, whereas if you don't pay a utility bill or a credit card they're unlikely to go all the way. That's why your mortgage is the first one to pay. I always try and set up mortgage direct debits within a couple of days of my wages or rent hitting my account because to me the mortgage is the most important bill I'll ever pay. A default on a mortgage payment is really bad – why would the bank give you another loan if you defaulted on your last one?

Say you didn't pay a Telstra bill even for only $50, you could cop a black mark on your credit file despite the small amount of money involved. When the bank runs your computer-generated credit check, it registers those black marks and makes you 'automatically invalid' if it doesn't like what it reads, which is probably any sort of default. They do this because the banks have the luxury of dealing with lots of customers, so they can handpick the best ones. If they find you haven't paid a bill, whether for $1 or $10,000, the bank would consider you to be some sort of risk compared to someone with a clean slate. The bank thinks – if you're going to default on $50, what's the chances on $200,000?

Because they're dealing with millions of customers Telstra and other billing agents have big systems and set procedures.

- One month late isn't too bad because you might be sent a *reminder notice*
- After two months they might send you a *second reminder notice*
- After three months they might send a third and final reminder threatening to take you to court if you don't pay.

Although at any point during those proceedings they could register that you haven't paid, it is usually at this final stage that they will put a default on your credit file, and they do so by registering your name with a company called *Baycorp Advantage* which administers all of this. Next, if you still don't pay, you will be summoned to court and if you lose the case it comes up as a 'court judgment' against you, which is even worse as far as your lender is concerned.

Maybe you were overseas. Maybe you are forgetful. Whether you can pay or not doesn't matter; from the bank's point of view that's all irrelevant. They're not saying you *won't* pay your bills, they're simply saying you're a greater credit risk than someone with no defaults. The bank doesn't want you to forget your mortgage commitments just because you are overseas, which is why it's useful to have all your regular payments on direct debit.

The black marks automatically come off after a period of time, but if you have a default notice it may affect you for 5–10 years, so they're not worth the hassle, not even if the other party is in the wrong. Even if you are in the right, sometimes it's worth paying that bill instead of fighting it. Even if you're arguing with a plumber over a bill, it suggests to the lender that it's easier for them to deal with someone who doesn't argue. If it's going to put the brakes on you making $10,000 or $50,000 a year through buying more real estate, it's not worth the hassle for a dispute about $200. A few years ago a lot of people argued with OneTel about their phone bills – and I was amongst them. I paid my OneTel bill immediately when I learned what an effect a default could make to my credit file. I figured that if it's the difference between me getting a home loan and not getting one, the personal cost of disputing a $200 bill wasn't worth the credit risk.

Mercifully there is some lenience. Certain lenders allow *one* default/ dispute. If it's your phone or utility bill the big banks may ignore a problem if it's under $200.

Paying bills on time is not something we always want to do, but if you let them run up you may find you have suddenly accumulated $5000 of bills, whereas if you pay them as soon as you get your wages, they come in bite-sized chunks. It may not be the most efficient way of doing it because the longer the money is in your account, the better for you. But paying bills first immediately cuts your spending because you won't have the money.

Correct Your File

Some credit history is good, nothing is bad, and too much is worse

If you've never had a loan in your life, your credit history will be zero, and the banks don't like that because (they say) if you've never paid off a loan you're a high risk (or an 'unknown quantity' at least) because you've never had a financial commitment. Whereas if you've had a mortgage or a car loan and you've paid the whole thing off, you've got a nice history which establishes that you've been able to pay $1000 a month for three or more years and that you have conformed to all the bank's requirements.

Some credit history is good, nothing is bad, and too much is worse.

Computers certainly can get confused. If you see a default or a bad credit history which you believe has nothing to do with you on your credit file – you can correct it. Go back to the company that's put the black mark on you and require them to prove that you owe them money. Tell them how, when and where they've got it wrong and get it sorted. It's always worth keeping all the relevant paperwork if you've had any bill disputes so if there's an argument further down the track (and everyone who handled your case in the past has now left the company in question) you can still argue your case to the new crew. Then make sure they communicate the error to *Baycorp Advantage* who hold your credit file.

Under these circumstances, you may want to inform your bank that there's a 'correction pending' before it checks your credit file. Maybe someone who doesn't pay his/her bills has the same name as you, or there may be other grounds for dispute. You can say, 'There's a black mark on my credit file, but here's a letter from *Baycorp Advantage* (or from Telstra, etc.) to show that it's a confusion over identity which is not me'. Do this when a human is looking at your details rather than a computer, because a computer-generated application only looks at data and cannot take such explanations into account.

Check Yourself Out

You can go online and apply for a copy of your credit file, and you can also monitor it so that every time someone runs a check on you, you'll get an email to that effect, which is essential for fraud prevention.

For example, if someone took a copy of your driving licence and started faking loans in your name, as soon as that person did so *Baycorp Advantage* would fire an email to you saying, 'This finance company checked out your file today' and they would state the specific purpose.

This would give you enough time to realise that you had not authorised them to do so, which would enable you to question the transaction. It is also worth receiving email alerts because if brokers are checking out your credit file without your authorisation you can also stop them.

Check it out for yourself (all information is correct at time of going to press):

- www.mycreditfile.com.au
- Go to 'order a copy of your credit file now'
- You can then click, 'My Credit File $23'. If you don't mind waiting 10 days to receive it by mail click on the 'free services' at the bottom of the page.
- If you want to register for the Credit Alert (which tells you every time someone checks your credit file) click 'My Credit Alert $30'.

Summary

Your credit file is a history of any money you have applied to borrow as well as a record of any times you have not kept to your promise of paying it back. It's important to pay your bills and loans on time as, if you don't, it gets harder and harder to borrow money from anyone else.

If you can't borrow money, it becomes very hard to buy property or anything else that will help you earn the money to have that ultimate lifestyle of which you have always dreamed.

ACTION PLAN

Log on to www.mycreditfile.com.au to get a copy of your credit file and subscribe to getting an email alert every time someone checks you out.

Go through your file (with a mortgage broker or accountant if necessary) and correct any adverse mistakes if they have any.

I commit to myself that I will pay every bill or loan on time as even the smallest error will affect my ability to borrow money in the future. It is not worth a $500 mistake to risk losing my dream.

chapter eight

Step Three: Face the Bank, or Your Broker

How do you get a mortgage?

Having worked out what you own and what you owe, and having also checked out your credit file to determine your standing in the eyes of your potential lender, you are now ready to approach lenders.

Times have certainly changed; 10–15 years ago, when you wanted to borrow money you'd go to see the bank manager and beg for a loan. Five years ago you'd deal with the bank staff who would advise you of the different products available. Now, rather than having in-house employees doing that job, many banks farm that work out to mortgage brokers who can arrange loans for you from a range of lenders.

Financial Portfolio

If you're organised and you know what money's going in and out, brokers and lenders will potentially have more confidence in you because they can see at a glance that you know what's going on. Whereas if you've got bits of paper everywhere, and you don't have a clue about your personal finances, they are going to be pretty nervous about lending you anything. If different facts come out each time they talk to you or if you start changing your story, they'll definitely become suspicious. You need to prepare a number of documents before you approach the banks or a mortgage broker.

Most of the bank staff are so used to lending money on properties that the system does it all for them, which is why they can approve or reject your loan within five minutes. The staff members are not there to make decisions, they are there to assist you – sometimes by answering questions, giving you brochures, showing you web pages and calculators and passing on other informational material.

Whoever you go to will want to see certain personal documents, which are probably right at your fingertips. Key documents they will want to see include:

- Birth certificate.
- Passport.
- Driver's licence.
- Marriage certificate (to prove a name change).
- If you own a property, the bank may wish to sight the rate notice to prove you still own it and in what name the property is listed.
- Your last two group certificates and payslips as proof of income.

Get all those documents in place before you do anything else and then it's easy for you to refer to them as necessary.

Mortgage lenders are there to make a profit. They want to lend money to people who can afford to pay it back; otherwise it costs them time and money to chase the debts. Bad debts ruin their reputation and affect them in other financial ways. Lenders also want to lend money on stable properties that could be sold in an emergency to pay back their loan. Therefore they have certain criteria which you need to meet before they will lend you any money.

Proof of income

Your income is sure to be one of the bank's main concerns. Not only do they want to make sure that you get a regular pay packet, they also want to make sure that you are in a stable job. They will get this information by asking for your last two payslips, your group certificates and/or your latest tax returns. Often, when you have just started a job there will be a three-month trial period which they may require you to complete before considering you for a loan.

Contractors and self-employed people often have more fluctuating incomes which makes lenders more cautious. Sometimes a letter from your accountant stating your last few years' income will be sufficient to keep them happy. There are also low doc loans now available which assist self-employed people by allowing them to self-declare their income. Because the bank is trusting their honesty, sometimes they charge a higher interest rate for these products.

Different banks will have different attitudes to certain particulars, but any income you can prove from any other source is useful, such as share dividends, second jobs or rents received.

Savings history

The bank will want to see consistent, regular savings

If you're buying your first property, the bank will want to see consistent, regular savings over a certain period. A bank is unlikely to give you a loan of $2000 a month if you spend all of your wages. It won't want to see savings of $10,000 one month, $5000 the next, then suddenly up to $15,000. It would rather see you put away $2000 a month over 10 months and not touch it. Because you won't be able to dip in and out of your mortgage, it doesn't want you dipping in and out of your savings account.

The bank is trying to ascertain whether or not you're capable of paying out $2000 each month. If you're already used to paying $1000 in rent per month, plus you have a program to save another $1000, it should be confident that if it lends you $2000 per month you've established that you've got the monthly resources and the savings habit to pay it back.

Interest rate rises and changes in circumstances

The bank knows that sometimes interest rates go up and it also knows that most people have sudden unplanned expenditure. Therefore when they calculate how much they are willing to lend you, they will add in a margin for your own protection. Even if you have $2000 spare out of your wages, the lender might assume that only $1500 of it is available for a mortgage payment.

Bank statements

The bank will want to check your last six months of bank statements. If you're going into overdraft every six months (and it's not part of your agreement) it is going to say to you, 'If you can't manage your wages each month, how are you going to manage a mortgage of a few hundred grand?'

Credit cards and personal loans

Your credit cards and other personal loans will also come under scrutiny. If you're not paying your credit card or car loan on time the bank is less likely to give you a mortgage.

A Fine Line

You are obliged to declare every single liability on the mortgage form, a lot of which are small factors. Getting a loan or not can come down to a very fine line; it's better to tell the whole truth from the outset rather than having the bank refuse your finance after you've bought a property, because of a small loan you never mentioned. They will find out.

Dependants

When the bank assesses prospective mortgagees it will want to know how many people are living in the household and how many dependants there are. To a banker every dependant is an extra liability. If the bank knows you've got a partner and four children it will say, 'You may *say* you only spend $1000 per month on living expenses but we have to assume you actually spend say $1800 because that's what the average family of that size spends.' And you're stuck with their figures.

Rental income

The bank may only count 75% of the rent as 'income'

If your income is largely derived from investment property rentals, the bank may only count 75% of the rent as 'income' because your tenants might move out and the property income would therefore go down until you find new tenants. Furthermore they may also add a margin to that because you'll have to pay for wear and tear, and possibly some renovations every couple of years.

Credit cards

Credit cards are a useful facility which enables you to draw out emergency money if something goes wrong. For example, if your water heater suddenly bursts and you need a quick $500 to spend on your property, a credit card is most useful to pay for those items. However, even if you don't owe anything on your credit card, the banks count credit cards as liabilities because they are a facility which enables you to instantly build up quick-and-easy debts. So in assessing your financial situation a bank will factor in the minimum repayment on each credit card. If the minimal payment is 3% per month the bank will assume that if you went out shopping and spent $10,000 you'd have to pay $300 back per month to service that debt.

- If you're going for a mortgage, one option is to pay off the balance then cut up your credit cards.

- Another option is to reduce the credit card limit to $1000 and then increase it later on if you find it necessary.

Other expenses

Some of the banks will ask you to estimate your monthly liabilities while others will determine the figure for you. So long as you're not making unsustainable claims the bank will reasonably trust you. Other times they will make their own assumptions. For example, if I wrote $100 a month as expenditure on a Ferrari (whether they are right or wrong in their calculations) they may say, 'Chris, maybe you spend a bit more than that…we're going to assume it's $1000.' Whereas if I've got an old banger that's worth $5000 (and in desperate need of repairs) and I say, '$100 a month', they might say, 'Fine, that's reasonable'.

Bank or Mortgage Broker

As long as you get the money, do you really care where it comes from? Generally not, and sometimes you need to go to different lenders depending on your financial circumstances and what you are trying to do.

As a broad generalisation the mainstream banks are great for the typical employee who has a permanent job in a solid company. When you are self-employed or have a bad credit history, sometimes you need to look further afield.

The Advantages of Dealing with a Bank

Some people see some kind of loyalty in dealing with the family bank, especially if they've been with it for 20–30 years, and often it's not just a money thing. They'll stick with that bank even though it's more expensive than the one down the road. It's certainly true of people like my parents who grew up in the days where they knew their bank manager personally, and who may also have come around to look over a property before they'd buy it.

Let me tell you, there is no such thing as a 'family' bank. These days it's all mass marketing. It's a lot of trouble to change banks, and the banks know it. An existing customer is less likely to make the effort to open an account somewhere else. Banks know that people like my parents will stay with them forever, so they are more likely to offer better deals to attract new customers than to take care of existing ones.

Better rate?

If you've held your account with a bank for a considerable time or they've got a couple of your mortgages, you may be able to negotiate a better rate. It can be difficult to negotiate with only one mortgage but if you've got 3–4 properties with the bank and you're threatening to take all your business elsewhere, they might cut you a better deal. But generally for your average mum and dad who are buying one property and only borrowing a few hundred thousand dollars, it's pretty hard to negotiate. If you're borrowing $200,000–$300,000 from a bank you think it's a lot of money, to them it's not a lot. They are probably doing millions of dollars a day.

It already holds your records

Your bank may already have a lot of information about you, saving you a lot of time in getting your payslips and tax returns together. They've seen your paychecks come in for the last 10 years, saving you the effort of providing your income statement. For people who don't like paperwork it may be easier to use your existing bank to get rid of those headaches. But never let that be the deciding factor because just by opening your eyes and looking around, if you can save a few hundred dollars each month for the next 25 years, it's worth going to the hassle of checking out all your alternatives.

Product knowledge

Because it only deals with a limited number of products (maybe 4–5 mortgage products) your bank knows each of them in detail and what additional costs may be applicable in certain situations. It's better to know upfront the costs of fixing, refinancing and breaking out of the loan at any point in time.

Disadvantages of Banks

Some of the disadvantages of going to a bank are:

Banks only recommend their own products

Banks only recommend their own products and that's a big disadvantage. A broker can evaluate all the lenders and all the options. The employees who work for the bank get paid because the bank gets the business. Sometimes you'll meet a friendly person who will say, 'We don't specifically handle that area but you can go and speak to this other place, whom we understand does a different kind of deal.' Just because one lender doesn't do it, there's always someone else that'll do it for a price.

Dealing with an employee

Sometimes when you are dealing with a large corporation, the customers only get to talk to the junior staff. If you are purchasing a home or a number of investment properties do you think you will get much direction from someone that may not have ever bought one? It all depends who you are dealing with.

If you have a high salary, private banking may be available to you. There you get a specialised team of advisers who are used to dealing with wealthier clients. They are more likely to make decisions according to your circumstances, rather than their standard procedures. In this case, these types of employees may work to your advantage.

Advantages of Mortgage Brokers

Number of lenders

The main difference between a bank and a mortgage broker is that a mortgage broker is normally free to take your business to any lending institution it wants. Even if you decide to use a mortgage broker it's worth doing your own research to see what's in the market. Check out the Net and the newspapers, then ring up and ask about their latest deals.

Another source of information is *Your Mortgage* magazine and other home buying magazines. They will often do your homework for you by researching 30–40 lenders and listing their conclusions, so it's fairly easy to check what's around. I'm suggesting you do this for your own edification, not to replace your mortgage broker, because the amount of time for you to learn in detail what 30 lenders can offer is too much, whereas brokers are dealing with it every day. They're just the middle people between you and the lender. Remember, you're borrowing money from the lender not the broker.

Sometimes brokers will charge you a fee but more often they'll get paid by the lending institution where they cut your deal. From a bank's perspective, paying a broker may be cheaper than the cost of having a full-time employee on staff. Rather than spending $100,000 a year to pay for that employee (inc. wages, car, phone, insurance and on-site costs) the bank may rather pay a mortgage broker a small percentage of every loan that is written. Typically the bank sets it up so that you get exactly the same deal if you come in through their front door or through a broker.

Range of product

One of the main advantages of mortgage brokers is that they have access to all lenders within the market and they should find the best offer based on what's good for you (rather than what's good for the bank). If you are getting the same deal from a broker as from a bank direct – why not use a mortgage broker and have someone onside working for you? If they can get the same deal from the banks as you, you haven't got a lot to lose.

More entrepreneurial

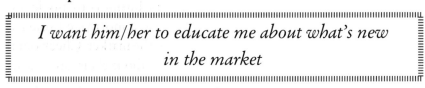

I want him/her to educate me about what's new in the market

Because brokers often don't get a wage and are usually paid on completed loans they may be more motivated to educate you about property investing so that you buy more properties which will then earn them more commission. Rather than me telling my broker what to do I want him/her to educate me about what's new in the market and to come up with new ideas I can use to make or save more money.

You might get a kick-back

Brokers get a fee for arranging the paperwork and giving your business to a lender. Some brokers may even agree to pay you a certain percentage of their commission back! They may say, 'Out of that $2000 – I'll keep $1500 and you'll keep $500', which could be another reason to use a broker rather than going direct to a bank. A lot of the banks don't think that's ethical practice and are trying to cut down on it. I wouldn't necessarily recommend going to someone who does that because that may persuade them to get you into loans that pay higher commissions rather than a loan you actually need. It's not necessarily a good thing – I only mentioned it to give you another idea of what's out there.

Calling home

Another advantage of using mortgage brokers is they usually come to your premises. Apart from the time-saving advantages this enables you to tell your story in your own space in your own way, with all documentation to hand.

Disadvantages of Mortgage Brokers

The disadvantages of using mortgage brokers are:

Less detail

Because they deal with so many lenders, brokers may only know the main highlights of each loan and not the detail. It is important to understand the ongoing costs and charges of the loan, not just the initial interest rate.

Franchise brokerage or one-man band?

There's pros and cons to everything, just because your broker is in a franchise brokerage (or is an independent) it doesn't mean they're any better than anyone else until you see what they can offer you. A franchise brokerage may have better systems and better disciplines if something does go wrong. You may prefer one brokerage over another or vice versa – it's hard to tell. It's like going to one branch of a bank compared to another branch. It's all the same bank, owned by the same people but your impressions all depend on whom you speak to. You may have more come-back if you're dealing with a big bank than with a one-man band who has given you wrong advice and put you into the wrong loan. An independent broker who has done the wrong thing may be hard to track down and even harder to sue.

Preferential treatment

Some of the banks pay different percentages to their brokers, so even though mortgage brokers say they're independent if they get 0.7% from one source and only 0.5% from another, they may be inclined to take you to the one who pays them the highest commission. (They are usually legally required to disclose their commission and the mortgage papers should state the amount your broker will be paid.) In reality, most salespeople concentrate on doing the deal rather than worrying about the difference in the commission rates, although that is a broad generalisation.

Special Circumstances

Getting a loan can be difficult, especially if you've got a special case which is when you need to talk to someone face-to-face rather than speaking to a tele-sales department. Applying for a loan on the Internet or over the phone may be fine if you've got a perfect savings history, a solid income and you're not borrowing much money. But if you're borrowing for the first time, sometimes doing it face-to-face is a lot easier because they can walk you through the process and if there's something different about you they can always make a special request to head office.

Certainly don't give up just because your local branch says no; there are a lot of other things you can do within that same banking system. Sometimes you might have to speak to a different person who understands your situation; other times you may have to go to a different branch. And sometimes the computers will come up with blatant errors.

For example, the percentage banks will lend sometimes varies with certain postcodes and you may be right on the border. In Sydney, there's a 'Hornsby-side' and a 'Wahroonga-side' of a suburb called Waitara, each having radically different socio-economic implications. Likewise, you may be in the right district with a postcode that's on the wrong side. So if you feel you have a case to argue, it's always worth talking to a different person, in this instance, someone who understands Sydney's upper North Shore.

Certainly if you're speaking to people in the CBD banks who are dealing with lots of applications, they may not have any time to give you any special service, whereas if you go to your local branch it may have someone with more time to look at your specific circumstances. This person might say, 'Normally we wouldn't lend in that area but because you've got a very good income – or because you've also got another property – we'll lend to you because of these special circumstances.'

If a farmer went to capital city mortgage brokers, the lender might say, 'That's too much grief, it's rural, I don't deal with that', whereas a mortgage broker in a rural locality will be much better attuned and more experienced in financing those kinds of properties. Furthermore, rural people are probably self-employed, so that broker is probably a lot better placed to help a self-employed person buy rural than someone from the city that sells lawyers into South Melbourne properties. He would know which particular lenders are used to those kinds of deals.

Age is another area of special circumstance, because the meaning of a 25-year mortgage to a 25-year-old fully employed person has far different implications than a 25-year loan to a 55-year-old person, whether that person is in full employment or not. 'It's easy for us to go out and buy a 25-year-old mortgage,' says Angus Raine, of the Raine & Horne real estate franchise. 'But when you're 50 the banks look at you completely differently.'

Don't get in over your head financially

Another area of concern is 'getting in above your head', according to John Symond of Aussie Home Loans. 'The level of housing debt in Australia, compared with incomes, is getting dangerously high,' says Aussie John. 'Buyers should be very careful to do all their sums with the help of a mortgage broker, so they choose the right loan for their needs and income levels. It is very important to consider contingency plans if you lose your job or some other problem occurs that makes servicing a mortgage too hard. Don't get in over your head financially. And seek professional advice from day one, especially in the area of how to comfortably service your repayments.'

Nevertheless he recommends making the effort: 'It can be difficult and time consuming to get into property ownership but you won't regret making sacrifices of your time and income as the rewards are usually great over the long term.'

So keep on trying. If someone turns you down, think through all the different ways of dealing with that situation. You might start by ringing up your local branch and you may finish up seeing a local broker. The point is, never give up. Just because one lender says no doesn't mean that's gospel! Even within that specific bank, if one person says no, talk to the top if you need to. If you've got a valid reason, keep moving from supervisor to manager to director.

Not All About Rate

Is the cheapest car always the best one? No. Is the loan with the cheapest interest rate the best one? Not always. Money from one lender is the same as money from another lender, so whoever lends it to you at the cheapest rate will probably get the best deal. However, there are other things to take into consideration.

How much will they lend you?

If one lender will lend you $400,000 at 6.5% and another will lend you $450,000 at 7% which is the better deal? Well, it all depends on what property you have in mind and whether you think that by buying a more expensive property it will grow more in percentage terms. Paying an extra 0.5% interest on $450,000 is just over $2000 a year which may be worth it if the property is likely to grow by $5000 extra.

What other costs are there?

Consider if you need to pay for each transaction that goes through your account or if there is a monthly account-keeping charge. How much would it cost you to cancel the loan after a year if you sold the property and how much would it cost to refinance the loan if you want to use the equity that you have built up.

Summary

There are pros and cons to using a bank or a mortgage broker and a lot of it depends on the person with whom you are dealing. Try going to both and then making your own decision.

Even though it is more fun to go looking for properties, it's pointless until you know how much a lender is willing to lend you. Rather than mark your credit file unnecessarily, ask for loan approvals in principle based on your financials until you actually find a property that you are interested in buying.

ACTION PLAN

Organise all your documents so that you are fully prepared to apply for a loan.

Ask friends and family if they can recommend you a good bank or mortgage broker. Ask them why they think they are good.

Go and see at least 2–3 banks/brokers so you can start to evaluate the differences. If you are looking at buying a number of properties then maybe you need to find someone that invests themselves so they can push you rather than the other way around.

Get an approval in principle or subject to credit check. If you get credit checked every time you see a new broker your credit file will be worth nothing.

SECTION B
GET SET

chapter nine

Step Four – Research the Suburbs

Investing time in research will create profits later

L ooking at properties at the age of 22 is quite a fun hobby, and I think a lot of people enjoy it, especially if they're planning to live in what they buy. Visualising how their life is going to change once they move into this new place is exciting. However, it's a big financial decision. It's tempting to jump into the first property you see but no matter how good the property you'll always find another one that's just as nice. The more time you take to research it properly, the more you will gain financially further down the track.

> *It's tempting to jump into the first property you see*

It's certainly the most expensive thing you will ever buy so it's not something to get emotional over. And it's pretty hard not getting emotional, especially if you've got a family, and the kids find a room that they want to turn into their bedroom before you've even made an offer on the house! Be emotional if you need to, but still keep a balanced financial perspective as there's a lot of money at stake.

I still get withdrawal symptoms going around looking at the various houses. Although I'm weaning off it more and more, I think you get involved in all of them, even investment properties. I got into them emotionally because I moved in for at least a year or two at the start – doing them up and moving on, whereas the last two I've bought are properties I definitely wouldn't live in, so there's been less personal attachment on my part.

> *The more research you do the better idea you have of what is good value*

The more research you do and the more properties you see, the better idea you have of what is good value and what is overpriced. It's well worth doing the legwork, because the more you speak to agents the more you will build your knowledge. You also build rapport which keeps you in the loop if the agent knows you are a serious buyer. And if someone is keen to sell, quite often 'quick sale' means they'll sell at a lower price. At this point the agent will not want tyre-kickers, only genuine buyers. If the agent knows you are keen, it's easy to call you and say, 'I know you're ready to buy, I've got this one you can get cheap, but you have to do the deal straight away.' That's happened to me, and always to my advantage.

The more properties they sell, the more commission agents make. That's how they make their money. They're working for the vendor and ideally they want to sell for the best price – it's good for the vendor, good for their sector, good for their business and good for their paypacket. At the end of the day no sale means no money, which is bad for all concerned including the vendor so, as a professional salesperson, agents will try to close the deal at any price in preference to letting it slip away. The difference in commission on a $400,000 sale is not much different to a $420,000 sale so they are just as keen to see you buy it.

Seller's market. In a market with lots of buyer interest, agents only need to get property onto the market and it'll sell. If it doesn't sell at auction it'll sell a few weeks afterwards. It's hard for a buyer to have much bargaining power in this market.

Flatter market. If it's the kind of market where clearance rates are around 50% it's harder for them to sell so they've got to spend more time trying to push the buyers. There's a greater chance of striking up a better deal.

Buyer's market. If things decline it eventually becomes a buyer's market where agents concentrate on trying to find buyers rather than properties. They may have listed 100 properties with no one to buy. In such a market the agent who's got a genuine buyer is the one who gets the money. And if you're a buyer in this market, you're holding all the aces.

What People Look for in a Suburb

Whether you're looking for a house to live in or as an investment, the same rules apply. But beyond the rules, you've got to pick what's right for you and there may be some things you'd consider important that may be different from what most people would want (like living near the bush and working from home makes being close to transport less necessary). Also proximity to schools becomes more important than public transport to parents who have to drive their school-age kids. All of these factors will constantly change as the family and the suburb changes.

Some of the things people take into consideration when they're looking at suburbs are as follows:

How close is it to work?

Most people want to travel perhaps half an hour to work, which suggests a band of suburbs roughly the distance you are prepared to commute. Are there plenty of other businesses that are close to the suburb in which you want to live, or is yours one of the few?

How close is it to public transport?

A lot of people travel by public transport so you may want to look for premises close to a train station and key bus routes that make it easy to commute into the city.

Check out the future

Take into account how your suburb is going to shape up in the future. Go to the local Council office and find out all the proposed development plans for residential, commercial and civic buildings. Find out who is buying into the area. The Australian Bureau of Statistics can give you a complete demographic breakdown, which lists average income per household, age, languages spoken, and all sorts of relevant data about the people in any suburb or location Australia-wide. A number of real estate websites will also provide suburb profiles although they may not be completely independent. Your solicitor or conveyancer can certainly check any development that will affect you. They will tell you if a proposed freeway is about to go through your property.

Locate where people like to be

I find that most people like to be close to parks, beaches, surf and leisure places. The chances are that if you are attracted to a property, then 'your type of person' will like it too, meaning that your taste is driving you into an area of like-minded people. For example, family people like to be close to other families. If the property is close to work, public transport, schools and leisure facilities it's going to be a family area – and hopefully other families will move in there as well.

Work out your driving cycle

Work out your shopping trips then try to pinpoint other key areas that you frequent in that locality. (The Rotary meeting place for Rotarians, the Methodist Church for Methodists, etc.) Plan to locate everything within a small area. You won't want to spend half an hour getting the kids to school and then driving off to work in the opposite direction.

Work out the investment cycle

Rod Cornish is Head of Property Research at Macquarie Bank. He believes that trendlines make some suburbs better investments than others. He says, 'Typically cycles spread and you need to see where we are on the cycle. In the late 80s, Bondi was a nice suburb, but it wasn't as desirable a place to live as it is now. There was a focus on building construction and then because it was undergoing a regeneration, wealth continued to move to the suburb. If you look back seven to eight years ago none of that had commenced. Bondi got up first, then Coogee followed some time later, then it flowed down to Maroubra. That all drives the median price up.'

> *It's hard for you to predict the future capital growth of the suburb*

It's hard to predict the future capital growth of the suburb but there are companies that specialise in providing research material to help in your decisions. Some of that information is independently sourced and some more biased to whatever they are promoting. Choosing a suburb that is predicted to grow at 12% should perform better financially than one predicted to grow at 6%. It may then come down to where you can afford to buy and if that's where you want to live.

Alternative suburbs

When buying their first property, a lot of people have got a suburb in mind where they want to live. It's best not to be too fixed in your ideas on location as you don't want to blinker-out other possibilities some of which may be advantageous if you are willing to make a small concession. It's worth coming up with a couple of alternative suburbs to use as a gauge. You may be able to buy a three-bedroom unit in one suburb for the same price as a two-bedroom unit in another. If you pick two suburbs instead of one, it'll double the opportunity of finding your ideal property or ideal bargain.

Once you've decided on a specific suburb an easy way to see what you can afford while sitting in your lounge-room is by going on the Internet or getting the local magazines, most of which have massive real estate spreads. Quite often you'll get wonderful pictures too, you'll certainly see the properties at their best! And most properties for sale have open times, which might be mid-week – say a Wednesday or a Thursday between 10.00–11.00am – and 10.00–11.00am on a Saturday.

On the Net real estate agents will sort properties into price categories so if you can afford $500,000 tops you can 'search' for properties between $400,000–$500,000.

When you see an ad for an auction property that catches your eye in a newspaper or magazine ring the agent and ask, 'Do you mind giving me an approximate idea of what it'll go for?'

Three Tips from Rod Cornish, Head of Property Research Macquarie Bank

1. Range. In terms of the information you've got, look at the whole range of properties and recognise the extremes so you know what to look for and what is 'reasonable risk'. Look at as much data as you possibly can, and look at what really drives the market long term.

2. Not quick. I recommend to anyone going into residential – do it for the medium to long term. A lot of people speculate but property isn't a speculative market, it's a market that you can't get in and out of quickly.

3. Generational shifts. Generation X for example has a different quota to Generation Y – who's driving the market? What sort of property will they increasingly want? Look at changing preferences and what that means – (smaller households?). People want to live closer to the beach. Obviously look at supply, you can see this very early if you look at Approvals.

Is it a home or an investment?

If you're buying your own house, it is sensible to look first at your comfort levels and those of your partner. There is often a certain idealism in this, but do try to bear in mind how supply and demand works, that house prices increase, and that clever buying now is going to set you up for the future.

No right and wrong

David Rees, Head of Investment Strategy at Commonwealth Bank offers some advice: He says, 'Don't buy an investment property in the same suburb as where you work. You should be diversifying geographically. If you're living in Lithgow and working in the Lithgow coal mines, don't buy a house in Lithgow. Think of it instead as a portfolio decision. Your job in the coal mines depends on the price of coal. Your house goes together with your job.'

As an investor who likes full tenancies, I'm always looking for something that's going to be good for the majority, and to me the majority of people would want something close to work, transport and the beach. I reckon Sydney is a good market because there's nowhere you can build to the east because of the sea and to the west you've got the demarcation of Blue Mountains. Within those two markers Sydney housing can only get more and more dense and I believe prices will keep moving up over the long term. However, as I buy more property I need to diversify into different areas so that all my eggs aren't in one basket.

There're no right or wrongs with these things, they're just items to take into consideration. For personal reasons, you may prefer to live in Bowral or Gosford and commute two hours to the CBD. I'm just sharing the way I think.

Summary

Buying property is a financial as well as an emotional decision. It's also a long-term decision. When choosing suburbs take the following into consideration:

- Proximity to work and public transport
- Future plans for the suburb
- Future capital growth

The more people who are attracted to that same suburb, the more property values are likely to grow.

Bernard Salt, Property Partner, KPMG Chartered Accountants, confirms our findings on growth suburbs. He advises foresight, knowledge and of course to stay close to the water. He says, 'Look for suburbs that will benefit from an imminent change in infrastructure. Think critically, talk to as many people as you can. And remember, anything on the water is good.' In line with population growth trends Salt adds by way of caution, 'Stay away from the dry flat wheat belt towns.'

ACTION PLAN

Pick 2–3 preferred suburbs.

Research websites and other sources to get background information.

Consider paying for independent research to get an idea of future capital growth predictions.

Buy a map of the local area and highlight schools, transport, parks, offices, water areas.

chapter ten

Step Five: Look for These Things in a Property

What are the important things to look for in a property?

Property is not my job, it's my hobby that happens to create an income and long-term wealth. I regularly check out properties on the Internet and I print out all the ones that interest me. Then I go through the magazines, cut out the properties I want to visit and build myself a map the day before open day, marking out my route. I do this because if there're a dozen properties to see between 10.00am and 1.00pm that probably only leaves 15–20 minutes per property at the max, so I need to save time driving around in circles to see as many properties as I can. I suggest you do the same if you want to take property investing seriously. Says Angus Raine, of Raine & Horne, 'I always tell my friends, if it's too easy there's something wrong. And that's the thing with property, you have to wear out some shoe leather.'

After you've seen so many properties it's so hard to compare one against the other, so I list everything I've seen and I write it up on a sheet of paper, then I transfer the information onto an Excel sheet to recall the details I could never have otherwise remembered.

I list:

- The address
- Estimated sales price, which is either in the ad or I ask the agent as soon as I walk in the door
- Number of bedrooms
- Whether or not it has a garage
- Whether it has balcony – or something like that
- Internal square metres
- External square metres
- Views – and whether they are view of the city, the harbour, the bush or the beach
- Expected auction date
- Name of real estate agent
- The actual selling price (get after it has been sold).

Scoring the properties out of 10 is particularly useful because it tells you at a glance the ones you liked and the ones you didn't. Scanning a copy of the flyer or advertisement into your computer and then linking it to an Excel sheet will make it even easier to analyse the properties at later date.

These days it's easy to take around a small digital camera for inside-and-outside photographs of every property to add to the ones on the agent's flyer. That made it very easy for me to make comparisons. If I saw a property for $500,000 and the next week I saw one that was virtually the same for $400,000, I'd know the second one was worth bidding on – and I'd have all the photos and the back-up evidence to prove it to myself.

Having a photographic memory isn't one of my strong points. Maybe it's the accountant in me, but documenting everything I see means I've got the most value for the amount of time I put into my research. All of my documents are still there; I go back to my notes because if a property gets resold a couple of years afterwards I can keep track.

Good Properties

> *The more properties you see the less time you generally need to spend in each one*

The more properties you see the less time you generally need to spend in each one. Because I've seen so many properties, after a quick look around I have a good indication as to whether or not it's worth going for. Sometimes I run in the front door and straight out the back, spending no more than two minutes on the premises. That leaves more time to spend in one that is worth the look.

According to Ron Switzer, CPA Australia, 'I think purchasing property depends on an individual's inclination for involvement with their investment. Some people like to touch and manage their assets. The appeal of various asset classes also depends on the objectives, needs and sophistication of the investor.'

> *Location-location-location*

Obviously everyone says the most important thing is location-location-location, so being in a nice area is obviously good. 'Would I be happy living there?' is the first question I ask. I might enjoy the street even before I walk into the property or I might enjoy the way the property is set out.

Here's what else I look for in a property:

Aspect

The main things I look for are generally light and heat. No matter how good it is in other ways, a property that is not well-lit turns me off straight away. I check that the main living areas are facing into the sun. In Sydney everyone is looking for north and north-east aspects because properties facing north-east are warmer and lighter, whereas the ones facing south don't have that advantage.

At the moment I live in a property that does faces south. Even though it's got amazing sea views I'm shivering in winter. Even though it doesn't cost much to heat the property I'm always walking into a cold house so it doesn't cheer me up straight away. But because the ocean view is so amazing it's worth it!

When I went up to Queensland to look at a property I noticed that Queenslanders are actually trying to avoid the sun. Because the sun is so hot up there they don't want something that's facing north-east and in direct sunlight. They want to block the sun. So that 'north-east' rule changes straight away depending on where you live.

Rent considerations

Properties that will always get a reasonable rent and are easy to rent out are very important to a property investor as it is the rent that pays the mortgage. The rent-return of above average properties (above the median price) tends to get less in percentage terms as the property price gets higher, and I have bought a few properties whose return in terms of rent aren't as good as they might have been. My strategy now is to buy around the median price because if 70% of the population can afford to live in it:

- I'll always have a tenant
- There'll be lots of other comparisons if I want to get the bank to re-finance it
- And there'll be lots of interest if I want to sell.

In contrast, if only 5% of the population can afford to rent something that's in the top end of the market, there's a greater chance of not being able to find a tenant and less chance of finding a buyer should the time come to sell. No tenant means no rent and no rent means an unhappy bank manager.

Good growth

> *The rule of thumb that I use is that property tends to double every 7–10 years*

The rule of thumb that I use is that property tends to double every 7–10 years. During that cycle it might flatten out, maybe even drop off a bit, then you might get 3–4 years of growth. So within that seven years you might get four years of growth and a three-year lull. According to that formula – if you had $1 million of property now:

- In seven years it'd be worth $2 million
- In 14 years it'd be worth $4 million
- In 21 years it'd be worth $8 million
- And in 28 years it'd be worth $16 million.

So $1 million worth of property now will be worth $16 million by the time I turn 65. Even if it doesn't go as quickly as those figures suggest and it's only worth half of that prediction, that's still eight million dollars, which – even given inflation – is a lot of money. I'm still pretty young and I've got another 30+ years until I'm 65, which is another four cycles. As long as I keep adding to my portfolio and the growth keeps ticking over I'm pretty happy and I shouldn't be short of a meal during my retirement.

If you think those figures are extraordinary why not do a poll of your parents' and relatives' properties where they have held them for 20–30 years. When I was four years old people were buying good-sized houses in the UK for $75,000 and 29 years later these places are now worth around $2m.

	5% growth	10% growth
7 years	$110,000	$150,000
14 years	$150,000	$300,000
21 years	$210,000	$600,000
28 years	$300,000	$1,200,000

So in this example that particular house has grown quicker than a doubling every seven years.

Just remember that because it has done it in the past there is no guarantee it will happen in the future. Ten per cent average growth also means that some properties may grow at 0% and some at 20% making an average of 10%. You've still got to ensure that you are buying property well to stay on the right side of the average.

Finding a property in a suburb that will give continual good growth is imperative to a property investor. Should you choose the ideal property that grows at 5%? Or should you choose a reasonable renter in a suburb that grows at 10%? Compound interest means that a suburb growing at 10% more than doubles the suburb growing at 5%.

I talk about property prices tending to double every 7–10 years quite often in this book, so have I got the figures to prove it?

The following figures are sourced from BIS Shrapnel and also include figures from the Real Estate Institute of Australia and the Australian Bureau of Statistics. I have taken their earliest historical figures and doubled them every seven years and then compared it to their actual figures. Over the last 35 years Sydney and Melbourne properties have come in almost exactly true to the rule and a few thousand dollars over. Brisbane started well, had a slower growth in the early 90s, and has been catching up by more than doubling in the last seven years.

Interpret the figures as you will.

Year to June	Sydney Actual	Sydney Doubling	Melbourne Actual	Melbourne Doubling	Brisbane Actual	Brisbane Doubling
1969	16,193	16,193	11,403	11,403		
1976	37,301	32,387	35,592	22,807		
1983	79,200	64,773	59,400	45,613	55,600	55,600
1990	181,000	129,547	150,000	91,227	110,000	111,200
1997	230,000	259,093	179,000	182,453	134,000	222,400
2004	520,000	518,187	371,000	364,907	306,000	444,800

Source: BIS Shrapnel, REIA, and ABS.

According to Commonwealth Bank's Head of Investment Strategy, David Rees, 'The decisions made by the average Australian since 1950 have been pretty good. If you'd known what you know now and put yourself in the position of the average Australian in 1952 and said, "Financially, what's the best thing I can do?" with the benefit of hindsight you'd have done exactly what they did – which is to buy a house. And that was a very smart financial decision. Anyone whose grandparents didn't buy a house would have lost out big-time.'

Not pristine

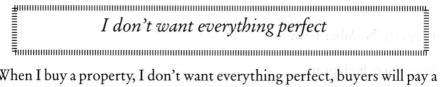

I don't want everything perfect

When I buy a property, I don't want everything perfect, buyers will pay a premium if everything's already done, there's nothing to fix and they can move in immediately because everything is absolutely pristine. Pristine commands top prices that I don't want to pay.

Seeing a place that's livable enough to rent out straight away but needs new carpets, repainting and maybe a new kitchen and bathroom is a real opportunity. I know that a lot of people won't want to do those renovations themselves and therefore they may not see the full potential of the house. Anyone with an eye for improvements can create additional equity, which is the difference between its actual worth and what you can make it worth.

In my first property I ripped up the carpets and re-varnished the floors. That took it into a different league. It took me eight years to change the kitchen and bathroom, but even before doing so, it was quite liveable and I always managed to rent it out.

Property number two needed no renovations but because I looked at it before it went on the market and felt that it was underpriced, I bought it at the price that they wanted.

The third property in Coogee was a paint and recarpet job three years later but because it had so much sunlight coming in, it was always going to be warm and welcoming from day one. As soon as I walked in the front door it looked good. The bathroom is still on my to-do list.

Property four had the potential to add on a third bedroom. This was a longer term project but its enormous potential made it well worth buying.

My fifth property was a house and land package in Queensland, where everything was brand spanking new. I bought it because the rent was a lot higher compared to New South Wales, and also because I got depreciation benefits because it was new. It was also in a high growth area so even if I'd paid market price I would still make a profit over the next few years.

Property Number 6 was off the plan and is still waiting to be built.

Equal-size bedrooms

Because I spend a reasonable amount of time in my bedroom watching television and relaxing after a hard day, bedroom size is important to me. If you're letting out a two-bedroom apartment to two single people you need two equal size double bedrooms.

Two-bedroom units often comprise one double bedroom and a smaller one that's really a single room. These days most single people want a double bedroom. No one wants the small room.

Built-in cupboards

Built-in cupboards are another good thing because these days no one wants to cart around a free standing wardrobe. If the unit hasn't got one I check for space to put it in, which is good enough for me because it's pretty cheap to have a wardrobe built-in, just a couple of doors and a few hangers.

Toilets, bathroom and en-suite

An additional toilet is always useful. Two professionals going to work at the same time will not have much patience if one is holding the other up. Toilets separated from bathrooms are good, so is one bathroom and an en-suite off the main bedroom. Ideally one person will use the en-suite while the other uses the bathroom.

Lock-up garage

Having a lock-up garage is very important. Most people who can afford $400+ rent don't want to park their car in the street.

To rent a garage currently costs between $30–$50 pw in the inner city suburbs which would easily add $50,000–$60,000 to a property. Apart from the increase in value, if you haven't got a garage some people won't consider your property at all. So if there's a choice of a $500,000 property without a garage or $550,000 with, even if you haven't got a car yourself consider whether you will have difficulty renting or selling the property in the future.

My Tamarama property hasn't got one, which could knock out maybe 50% of its marketability to tenants. It's close to the beach so I think it will always attract tenants but 'no garage' certainly comes up as an issue. Luckily for me most of the properties in that area don't have garages either and as it's such a small suburb new tenants don't have too many choices when something becomes available. I'm still happy with the property, I think it has other advantages despite not having a garage.

Open House

When you go into an open house you will often find a real estate agent at the front door asking for your name and contact details. A lot of people find this confronting but it's an advantage if you're genuine. The agent is only trying to keep a log of everyone who's been through the property so that the agency can keep the serious buyers informed. They might phone you up and say, 'We've got a potential buyer at $500,000 before the auction, are you interested in bidding as well?' Without the agent knowing that, you're not in the race.

As well as the agent on the door there's usually another milling around asking and answering questions and trying to gauge people's interest. It may be worth building rapport with these people and also trying to find out a bit more about the property while doing so. You may find out that the vendor has bought another property and is under pressure to complete the deal.

The agent often hands out an A4 flyer with the main details of the property listed and quite often a floor plan is printed on the back showing the exact sizes of the rooms. This is all useful information especially when you're back home trying to remember what you've seen – 'Did the second bedroom face east or did it face north?'

I usually scribble a few notes on that flyer.

Three Tips from Anthony Bell, Director, Bell Partners, Chartered Accountants

1. High demand areas. I'm looking at places that have a good infrastructure, local community stuff like police stations, close to transport, harbourside/waterside.

2. Personal opinion. Ask yourself, 'Is this the kind of place I'd actually want to rent and live in?' If I were a renter and not a buyer, would I want this place?'

3. In-demand areas. Prefer coastal, beachside, parkside areas where tenancy will always be reliable.

Summary

We've established that buying property is a long-term strategy and so you need to make sure that you buy the right property in the first place. Put yourself in the shoes of a renter and see if it is something that you would want to live in.

To find the best property at the best price you've got to do some legwork and there's no short cut. Many established investors and buyer's agents may see 50–100 properties before picking the right one. It may sound like hard work but if you can save 10% on the cost of a $500,000 property, that's $50,000 saved for a few weekends' effort and just think of how fit you got too!

ACTION PLAN

Cut out the adverts from the papers and plan a route for the following day based on the opening times.

Make a list of all the properties you see as it will help you to evaluate what is a good price or not.

Also write a list of all the important factors that you want in your ideal property and then agree which ones are imperative and which are optional extras.

Go and wear out some shoe leather.

chapter eleven
Property Number One

Borrowing $175,000 at 22 when your salary is only $25,000 is not most people's ideas of a good bet. When you realise the annual mortgage payment of $27,500 is more than your wages before tax, it is certainly not something most people's parents would approve of either.

I took on that bet with my first property and with hindsight have realised an average return of $50,000 a year over the following 11 years. I didn't make that bet because I was clever, I made it because I wanted the freedom to move out of home.

Sarah, Tim and I were brought up with the philosophy that you should own your own home rather than renting ('rent money is dead money', as they say). At the age of 21 I had just come back from Australia. I wanted to get out of home, and the ideal thing was to buy my own property. Having curfews and being told when to come in at night really motivated me to get my own place. That's when I started looking at open houses.

When we were younger, Sarah, Tim and I inherited $50,000 each which we were only allowed to use for investment purposes. It was good that my parents had disciplined us with that condition as no doubt I would have spent mine on having a good time. Sarah used her money as a deposit on a house and so I started thinking along the same lines.

As soon as I saw the first property my mind starting visualising the freedom and fun I would have if I owned my own place. Those all night parties, friends staying over, eating and drinking whatever we wanted, no one to tell me what to do – pure paradise! Once a dream is firmly lodged in my head – be it a car or a house or something else – I get motivated to do whatever I have to do to get it.

That first property I saw appeared to be perfect – it was in the city and it would have been ideal for having friends round. I was tempted to buy the first property I'd gone to see. But I can't even remember it now as I didn't buy it. It probably wasn't even that nice but I wasn't looking for the best investment. A property equalled freedom, so any property would have done. My emotions were flying and I could have ended up anywhere.

Luckily enough I kept looking and the more places I saw, the more my dreams got bigger and bigger, a bit like the champagne lifestyle but on a beer budget. I started playing around with the figures to find any way that I could to justify buying the dream house that I couldn't afford. And that's what it's like if you have a dream that you really believe in, you will make it happen.

The more properties I saw the more I started to realise that nothing was really hitting me in the face and saying, 'This is perfect.' Suddenly I saw this place, which I thought was amazing. It was owned by an Indian doctor and had a welcoming smell of burning incense as soon as I walked in. It had high ceilings and polished floorboards which gave it an overall appeal of a classy executive apartment.

I knew I couldn't afford the repayments but I was desperate for it so I put an offer to the estate agent. I said that I was really keen and that all I could afford on my wages was $185,000 and that was pushing it. Someone obviously outbid me as I heard nothing from the agent, which is where this story should end. I certainly thought I'd lost the house.

In the UK property deals work in chains – someone has to sell their house to pass the proceeds on to another person who can then pass on the proceeds to the person that they want to buy a property from and so on. The doctor I was trying to buy the house from had already bought the property next door in anticipation of the sale and was desperate to complete in time as the bank would not lend him the money for both properties. Unfortunately for the person who had outbid me, his chain collapsed which meant that the doctor no longer had a buyer and so it came to the point that he had to sell the house no matter what.

Being a first home buyer I wasn't involved in any chain, so one day the estate agent rang me up and said, 'Chris, the house could be yours but you've got one chance – you've got to put up the most money you can and we'll have to sell it to the doctor based on the fact that you can exchange immediately.'

By that time I think my wages had risen from $20,000 to $25,000 but even so it was a lot of money for me to be spending. I made a final offer of $200,000 and said that I only had $25,000 deposit meaning that my mortgage of $175,000 was going to be seven times my income rather than the three times that banks normally lend. For that reason I could not offer them another cent.

They knew the property was worth $250,000, so did I, but at the end of the day if they didn't get the property sold, the doctor was going to lose his dream house next door. There was no one else in the queue so I became his saving angel.

> *I had to convince my Dad to underwrite a mortgage that was seven times my income.*

With the banks only wanting to lend me $75,000 I was still $100,000 short. I knew it was a lot of money but I also knew that I was doing the right thing. My father was the only possible avenue for money. I knew he wouldn't give it away, but I thought I could maybe persuade him to go guarantor if it looked like a reasonable deal. At first, this didn't seem possible. After all, I had to convince my Dad to underwrite a mortgage that was seven times my income.

So I had to think creatively.

Numbers Game

I started fiddling around with the numbers. That's where I find all my best answers. I could see that I really needed to buy this three-bedroom house and not a one-bedroom unit for $125,000.

I could obviously see that a three-bedroom house was going to be much more valuable than a one-bedroom unit. The first reason was that a $125,000 property that rises by 10% pa would make me $12,500 pa whereas if this property rose by the same percentage I'd be getting $25,000 pa – double.

> *A three-bedroom house would actually be cheaper than a one-bedroom flat!*

The second thing that seemed to make sense, when I analysed the figures, was that if I bought a one-bedroom place it would cost me $500 per month which was the kind of money that I could barely afford by myself given that I was paid $850 before tax. But if I could somehow manage to buy this three-bedroom house instead – it would cost maybe $900 per month – and if I could rent out two rooms, it would effectively cost me nothing. Therefore, despite the massive mortgage, a three-bedroom house would actually be cheaper than a one-bedroom flat!

Young professionals have got money. If you've got a professional person in each bedroom (for example, an accountant and a lawyer) they can generally afford to pay well and on time.

Property Type	1 Bed	3 Bed
Property Cost in 1992	125,000	200,000
Less deposit	25,000	25,000
Mortgage	100,000	175,000
(2 Mates @ $375/mth)		750
Less mortgage/mth (interest only @ 6.25%)	521	911
Cost to me per month	521	161

Even though Sarah, Tim and I come from exactly the same background, we all have completely different attitudes towards money and debt. Sarah is reasonably conservative and risk averse and therefore she didn't want a large mortgage and will do whatever she can to pay it off.

> *Being in debt from the day I left school made me more open to the idea*

Being in debt from the day I left school made me more open to the idea and, as I had already jumped in at the deep end with other loans, I wasn't too fussed when it came to having a big mortgage. The numbers stacked up and so the decision was made. I had no knowledge about the future property market. I just assumed it would always go up.

My brother Tim is four years younger so he was too young to do anything with his inheritance money at that time, though he did buy a property a few years later. His attitude to money is similar to mine in that he is good at spending it and also happy to borrow for a good investment. Maybe this book will set off a dream for him to buy some more properties.

I was an accountant at the time, my salary was going up, I had tenants paying me rent and my Dad was guarantor. With all those three factors in place, I reasoned that there was a good chance that this property was a safe bet. In the end my father stood by me. I bought the house with a $25,000 deposit and a $175,000 mortgage, so I bought it for $200,000 and at least 20% less than it was worth. Without really realising, I had just made $50,000 – two years' wages overnight

I don't believe in trying to push someone if they're in a bad situation

I don't believe in trying to push someone if they're in a bad situation. The main reason I never feel guilty about buying at a knockdown price is they wouldn't sell it if they weren't ready to do so. If they want to give me a discount – it's a good thing, thanks. The doctor had already bought the house next door and had to settle fast. He wanted the house next door so much that he was prepared to risk losing money, which he did. If I'd offered $150,000 he wouldn't have taken it. Any deal has got to be acceptable to both parties and there's always a figure in between.

The previous buyers said they'd pay him $250,000 and when the chain fell over his best opportunity was to come to me. I could only afford $200,000 and that's the price we agreed. I physically couldn't pay any more and he had to sell the property.

In reality he had bought the house many years before for probably $100,000 and so rather than taking a heavy loss he just wasn't maximising his profit. He got his dream house, so did I and we've been great neighbours ever since.

I literally chucked in every last cent I had to come up with my deposit and costs, fortunately the property started generating money as soon as I got tenants in. I started renovating it myself but that didn't work so

I let a mate live rent-free for three months to help me renovate it. It all improved the investment. In fact the rent from two friends was almost paying the mortgage.

Analysis of purchase

> *You are more likely to find a bargain when you look at 100 properties rather than just one*

- Inspecting 80–100 properties gives you a better understanding of what is available and what each property is worth. You are more likely to find a bargain when you look at 100 properties rather than just one

- Analyse the numbers to make sure you can afford the property. Even having one tenant paying the rent made it as affordable as buying a one bed unit

- Signing an agreement subject to finance, valuation and building inspection allowed me to make offers that I wasn't financially committed to until all the checks had been done. It gave me flexibility.

Changes I would make with hindsight

Getting an offer of finance from a bank or mortgage broker prior to searching will ensure that you don't waste time looking at properties above or below your price range. In this case it worked though as I managed to stretch my finances.

Immediate Renovations

With a full-time job and having to study at night, I didn't have much free time to paint and renovate a new house. So for $5–10/hr I got my brother and a friend to rip up the odd bits of carpet, sand all the floors, revarnish them, strip wallpaper and do all the stuff like that.

I was starting to learn to delegate and – wanting to earn some pocket money – my poor little brother Tim was pretty useful. A lot of it was cosmetic like painting and re-sanding. I didn't put in a new kitchen until I moved to Australia, which I kick myself for because I had a bad kitchen and bad bathroom all the time I lived in there and nice ones after I moved out!

Good Profit

That first St Albans property has since increased from $200,000 to $750,000. The $25,000 I was earning in the UK then would be maybe $50,000 now – so wages have doubled, but the property has almost quadrupled! However, rents haven't really changed much over the past 10 years, they have gone from roughly $2000 to $2500 per month. With the rising house prices, rent has done the opposite and has effectively gone from 11%–12% return down to 4%–5% return. Hopefully the rents will start catching up!

My mortgage on that property is now $550,000. So as the house went up in value I have gone back to the bank, refinanced, taken the equity out, got a bigger mortgage and used the money to reinvest in other places.

Keep reading for more details on refinancing ...

chapter twelve

Step Six: Get a Valuation

Protect yourself

Even after you've done your homework, collected your clippings and run around on a Saturday looking at property after property, you still may not be an expert in all the areas in which you're about to invest. That's why you need someone to independently value anything on which you are going to bid or make an offer.

Just like people hire the services of professional art or antique valuers, there are also real estate valuers. The valuer takes an overview of the market and makes comparisons of similar properties that have been sold. Because the valuer has been independently hired by you, s/he is answerable to you. Not only can s/he confirm a fair price, your valuer can also confirm that it is potentially a reasonable investment. Any faults s/he finds in the property are also very valuable negotiating points that you can take to the seller or agent.

A few hundred dollars is a small price for an effective insurance policy

A few hundred dollars – especially when you're buying $400,000–$500,000 properties – is a small price for an effective insurance policy of a professional second opinion.

When you go to a bank to get a mortgage, the bank will usually send out its own valuer and, because it hires the valuer (albeit on your behalf), it won't necessarily tell you the findings. The funny thing is *you* actually paid for that service! The bank hired the valuer out of your money. Nevertheless, a bank valuer reports to the bank, not to you.

Even though there are a lot more regulations these days, there have been occasions when some banks realised that properties were being undervalued and they still didn't tell the customer. This was part of the Queensland two-tier marketing fiascos of the 1990s. This is what occurred.

Let's say for instance that you owned a $500,000 property and you had virtually paid off the whole mortgage. You went to your bank and said that you wanted to buy a unit for say $300,000. The bank might have said, 'We will give you 100% finance on the new one as long as we have security over both.' This you agreed to.

From the bank's perspective they were lending $300,000 on two properties that were worth $500,000 + $300,000 = $800,000. They were happy.

However, it all went bad for you when the undisclosed bank valuation of the second property came in at only $250,000. The bank thought to itself, 'Well we have got $500,000 + $250,000 = $750,000 security for our $300,000 loan. We're covered!'

Many customers like you did not realise that you had overpaid for your properties until it came time to sell. Even years later some of the properties are still not worth what you paid for them.

My ultimate rule for investing in property is always get an independent valuation

My ultimate rule for investing in property is to always insist on seeing the bank valuation figure and even better to *always* get an independent valuation from someone not recommended by the bank, the seller, the real estate agent or anyone else connected with the sale. This is almost a guaranteed way of making sure you're not getting ripped off on the price at least.

Different Types of Valuations

Drive-by valuations are often bank-paid and are named that way because the valuer will often drive by without even stopping. How can such a valuer tell how good the views are or whether or not the apartment is well kept? If you have an apartment in bad condition the valuer might give it a higher valuation than normal and if it is pristine condition it might be lower than normal as s/he will be taking an average figure.

A **full valuation** is where the valuer inspects the inside of the property and therefore gets a better idea of its current condition. The valuer will take into consideration the size in relation to other apartments and also the views. On the negative side they may consider any traffic noise and anything else that may detract from attracting tenants or buyers when the time comes for renting or selling the property.

Jason Field, Director, National Property Valuers New South Wales, defines **market value** as: 'the best price at which the property being valued might be expected to be sold at the date of valuation assuming:

- A willing but not over-anxious vendor and purchaser
- A reasonable period in which to negotiate the sale, taking into account the value of the property and the state of the market
- The value will remain static throughout that period
- The property will be freely exposed to the market
- No account will be taken of any additional bid by a special purchaser.'

Quite often valuations are reasonably conservative and so if you pay within a valuation price you should not be overpaying. Often bank valuations can be done on a fire sale basis which means that they are valuing on the basis of finding a buyer very quickly – obviously at a lower price.

When I use the services of the valuer I specifically ask for a 'full valuation' which means the valuer has got to:

- Go inside the property
- Sight every room
- Measure up and compare it to other properties that s/he's seen
- Provide me with a specific estimate, detailing the other property comparisons.

Don't Be Afraid to Turn Down Opportunities

S/he who has the gold makes the rules

Don't be afraid to turn down opportunities. Even though they might look good, they're not all for you. Remember your goals? Remember what you wrote down about what you like and don't like about certain properties? Don't let anyone turn your head. Never forget the Golden Rule, 'S/he who has the gold makes the rules' and if you've cleared yourself with the bank, you've got the gold. Suddenly all these real estate agents want it. This is where an independent valuer becomes indispensable.

Because everything I'd bought in Australia was in Sydney's eastern suburbs, I looked at diversifying my property portfolio, so I looked at some properties in Parramatta through an investment group who took me out on a Saturday morning and showed me around. They were getting investors like me out of central Sydney and taking us out west where property suddenly looked cheap, hoping we'd sign up because we'd think they were bargains.

I have a fairly good idea of what properties are worth in Sydney's eastern suburbs, whereas there is no way I have much of an idea of what property should sell for elsewhere.

These investment clubs take you out themselves. All you see is what they show you, you don't see any other agents nor any other properties, and under such circumstances I cannot proceed without a valuer. I went to see this place which certainly looked like a nice property. Compared to eastern suburbs prices of $500,000–$600,000 for a two-bedroom unit in Coogee, $450,000 for a three-bedroom house in Parramatta looked pretty good value. But my valuer said no. He said, 'It's only worth $400,000. It's $50,000 over-priced and it's on a main road. There are plenty of other properties in quieter streets going for less – walk away.' Walk away – I did.

Another time a Melbourne investment group was trying to sell me a serviced office – a shell of an office that has a central secretary and boardroom facilities that you rent out on a short-term lease just like residential property. Again, rather than spend $500 on a flight to Melbourne I simply paid a valuer $500 to do two hours research. He came back with the answer, 'All the information the investment group has given you is well out of date – possibly two years old – the market in Melbourne has changed and it's definitely not worth it.' That was the end of that.

Challenge the Agent, Challenge Everyone!

'We've already sold three of them at $450,000'
– doesn't mean it's worth that figure

Even if the agent says, 'We've already sold three of them at $450,000, look, we've got a copy of a valuation', that doesn't mean it's worth that figure. It means they've ripped three other people off for $450,000 and they have a cooperative valuer who will follow their instructions and write out their price!

With just a little bit of knowledge you can suddenly turn the tables on these hustlers and know straight away what the situation is, what their knowledge is and what they're really doing in the business. I challenged the guy who was trying to sell me the Parramatta property and said, 'You're not offering me a cheap property. It's $50,000 overpriced, I've had it valued' and suddenly the way he talked to me completely changed. Whereas before he was saying, 'We're giving you a competitively priced property…' and all the rest of it, he now went on the defensive. He said, 'Oh well, we're not trying to sell cheap properties, we're trying to sell you a complete service which obviously comes at a price.'

I said, 'I've already got four properties. I don't need that help and I'm certainly not paying $50,000 for it.' And that was the end of our business. Losing $50,000 on deals like that is very easy yet it would only cost you $300–$400 to double-check it. Think of a valuation as part of the cost of buying, it's just the cost of doing business.

A lot of people wouldn't spend that $300–$400 on a valuation because they'd think, 'If I don't buy it I've wasted my money.' But even if you did it 10 times and it cost you a total of $3000–$4000 before you bought a property – you couldn't count it as a loss. If you're going to risk $300,000–$400,000 buying a property, $300–$400 is only 0.1%.

Even if you have bought in the best growth suburb for the next few years, if you pay 10–20% too much for your property it's going to take the market a couple of years of growth to get you back to where you started. Surely it's worth investing some time and effort to make sure you're not taking a backwards step.

However, having said that, some effort is better than no effort. Even if you have overpaid, at least you are likely to make a profit some time. Compare that to those who just talk about it and never take any action, they'll never make a profit. A loss now but some profit in the future has got to be better than no profit, ever.

Summary

Getting independent valuations is a sure-fire way to minimise getting ripped off and paying too much for a property. For the valuer to be independent s/he can't be recommended by anyone connected to the sale. Make sure your valuer carries adequate professional indemnity insurance in case they make a mistake.

The best additional insurance is to make sure you've done your legwork. I have seen plenty of comparable properties go for higher prices.

ACTION PLAN

Ask friends, colleagues, or ideally, other property investors for names of independent property valuers. Alternatively look in the Yellow Pages for a specialist in the area.

chapter thirteen

Property Number Two

Half a million dollars in property on a $25,000 salary sounds like a hard ask, but – as they say – 'where there's a will, there's a way'.

A year after buying my first St Albans property, I was bored again and I felt like going shopping. But rather than doing the retail therapy that most people do, I thought I would go shopping again for property. I didn't really have much money and was sure the bank wouldn't come to the party but since when does lack of money stop most people when they engage in other types of shopping?

Dangerous Game

I was still in contact with the real estate agent who'd sold me the previous property and I told her that I was still interested in the market. By chance, and because we were friends, she happened to have another property that had just been renovated and was about to go on sale. She had the rights to sell all four in a converted house.

She thought it had been priced very low but the owner was keen to sell quickly and would prefer not to have a long drawn-out marketing campaign. She told me, 'It's priced at $200,000 – and I suggest you take it because if you offer less someone else will buy it straight away.'

> *I had to come up with a plan about how I was going to buy a second $200,000 house with virtually no money down*

It was another under-valued three-bedroom unit in St Albans – close to the station and good for commuting. I walked in and thought it was amazing straight away. It was very similar to the one I had previously bought, but had three larger double bedrooms and much more usable space. So five minutes later I said, 'Fine, I'll take it at $200,000.' Even though I didn't have a mortgage and didn't have anything arranged, I wanted that property because I recognised a bargain. So I said, 'I'll take it but I'll need a couple of days to sort things out' which is when I had to come up with a plan about how I was going to buy a second $200,000 house with virtually no money down.

Offering to buy property without having the finance in place is a dangerous game as you can be legally forced to complete on any agreement, and must wear the consequences. In the UK at the time you could agree to buy a property and even sign an agreement but it was not legally binding until the finance was in place and the solicitors had settled the deal, often six weeks later. Probably by luck rather than good judgement I was doing the right thing. Under Australian law there is no cooling off period with an auction so you must ensure that your finance is in place before making a bid. Where properties are for sale by private treaty, you can make them conditional on being approved for finance.

I had to start researching how to get a second mortgage – fast.

I had two things in my favour, and time was not one of them. My previous property had moved up in value plus I still had $12,500 of my inheritance money left. I thought, 'That's a start but I need a lot more money to get into it.' It was a bit of a wing and a prayer to put it together on my part. I only had a few days to sort it all out and sign the papers.

There was no way the banks would lend me money on the strength of my financial position so I came up with a plan of how to sell the idea to my dad. This time we would invest together, not with him as guarantor, but in partnership. I knew he would have to put up the majority of the money and would be raising the joint-mortgage, so he would be giving that side of the deal. My side of the deal was that I found the bargain which would probably give us an immediate profit of $50,000 and I was prepared to do absolutely all the work. This was in 1993, exactly one year after I bought the first one.

Some people don't want to ask their parents for help

Some people don't want to ask their parents for help and they don't want to take it to their friends, but this is a good example of where it worked for both parties. I think it's okay to approach a friend, relative or colleague and say, 'I've got the information that can make us a lot of money. Let's go in together, if we lose money we're losing 50/50 and if we make money we'll split it 50/50.'

I rang Dad up one night and said, 'I've thought of a plan of how we can invest together, how we can both put a bit of money in and both make some money. I think it's a good idea.'

He said, 'I'm listening...'

I said, 'I've already made money from the property I bought last year so why don't we do it again? I'll find the property and do all the negotiation because you work long hours. I'll look after the property, maintain it and get the tenants. You won't have to do anything.'

He said, 'I'm happy to look at the idea and how about we take it from there?'

So I replied, 'Well, it just so happens I saw one just yesterday, it's an absolute bargain and we've got a couple of days to make a decision if we really want it.'

And it all went from there – he inspected the property the next day, we approached the bank for a joint mortgage and we started learning about investment properties and how to get tenants in.

I guess my understanding of numbers made me come up with this deal.

My financial proposition was:

- We need to borrow $200,000 from ourselves and from the bank. So to make it fair why not pay ourselves interest on whatever money we each put in at the same rate that the bank charges us? Then as far as the property accounts are concerned we'd pay – say – 7% interest no matter who provided the funds.

- We'll get three tenants in as soon as possible which should generate $1875 per month.

- Any remaining profit we'll split 50%/50%.

Would you take this deal?

Would you take this deal? 'Rather than you getting 3% in a savings account I'll double your money and pay you seven. So if the mortgage rate is 7%, I'll pay you 7% of your money out of the profit we make on whatever money you put in. And whatever money I put in I'll pay myself 7%. The rest of the money we'll borrow from the bank.'

The day we bought that second property for $200,000, it was probably worth $225,000–$250,000.

Analysis of purchase:

- Property purchased at $50,000 under value due to relationship with estate agent and buying before it went on the market.

- Finance arranged with joint venture partner by paying 7% return on their money and splitting the capital gains. I found the deal, managed the process and found the tenants to make it easier on the joint venture partner.

- The property was already in pristine condition but represented good value as the seller was after a quick sale and was not up to date with his comparisons of market value.

Changes I would make with hindsight:

- Not having finance arranged beforehand made it more stressful to complete. When a great deal comes round you have to be ready to act.

Apart from the initial work involved in buying the property, sorting the finances and getting tenants to move in, this investment has been pretty passive. As it had been renovated at time of purchase, we are now only just looking at repainting the interior 11 years later.

The property has risen from $200,000 to $650,000 in about 10 years which is a profit of over $40,000 pa. A small deposit, a few weeks' work and checking that the rent has been paid once a month creates a reasonable passive income, don't you think?

As tenants, we got three student accountants who paid us $1875 a month between them straight away. Our mortgage and payments to us on $210,000 at 7% was only $1200 per month interest only. So we were jointly pocketing $600+ per month from the start.

Rental income/mth	$1875
Mortgage/mth ($210,000 @ 7%)	$1225
Profit to me/mth	$650

If you want to buy property but haven't yet done so, why not write down a list of the reasons why you haven't and then analyse them to see if they are valid or mere excuses. If one of them is that you are too busy, fast forward and then look back over your life at the age of 65. Could you say to your grandkids I never really became financially successful because I was too busy!

SECTION C

GO FOR YOUR LIFE!

chapter fourteen

Step Seven: Get Comfortable at Auctions and Private Treaties

The pros and cons of auctions/private treaties

When you're buying property there are generally two types to look into: properties that are for sale by private treaty and properties that are to be sold at auction.

As large amounts of money are being thrown around the room, auctions can be pretty scary places if you've never been to one and if you don't know what you're doing. The only way to get comfortable is to attend lots of them to see how the actual process takes place.

The more different venues you go to as an observer, the better you will perform. If you don't understand what's going on, the agents will gladly explain because they know the more confident you are, the happier you will be about bidding. If you're too nervous to bid, the agent knows you won't.

The Process

Auctions are sometimes held in the house or unit under the hammer and other times in big auction rooms (often a converted conference room) where the agent will sell about 20 on the one night. Auctioning them on site only draws out the interested parties whereas auctioning them all together draws a bigger crowd and creates more excitement, which might raise the individual bids.

Everyone intending to bid is required to show ID and register themselves on the day. Each person is assigned a paddle with a number on it so that the auctioneer can recognise who is bidding. This is an attempt to stop 'dummy bidding' which is a dubious practice whereby some sellers would get their family and friends to pretend early interest in certain properties to force genuine buyers to increase their bids.

Stick to Your Guns

The seller will have a 'reserve price' for the property. This is the minimum price for which they are willing to sell. If the bids don't reach that price the property remains with the vendor and if the bid does go over that figure then the highest bidder becomes the purchaser, and then the owner.

The auctioneer will address the crowd and describe the key features of the property about to be auctioned. S/he will also briefly describe the contract that the winning bidder will be required to sign on completion of the bidding process. The auctioneer will also go through specific details of the law which relate to bidders not being entitled to cooling off periods, as may be conventional with other kinds of offers. The auctioneer will also state that if the reserve price is not met then the property will be 'passed in' after which the highest bidder will have the opportunity to carry on negotiations with the seller if he or she elects to do so. The bidding then begins.

The crowd will be tense as the auctioneer asks for an opening bid. If all remains quiet s/he might suggest a price and say something like, 'Who will give me this amount?' Bidding normally starts from there and goes up in regular amounts such as $10,000.

At this stage you are welcome to bid whatever you want. Just raise your paddle and either say the amount you want to raise the bid by ($10,000) or state the full amount you want to bid ($430,000). Rather than saying four hundred and thirty thousand dollars, you can normally say '430'. Quite often the auctioneer will repeat and confirm the amount which you should correct immediately if there has been any misunderstanding.

> *The auctioneer's job is to keep excitement in the room running hot*

The auctioneer's job is to keep excitement in the room running hot and to build up the amounts people are bidding. If things go quiet s/he will tend to push the interested buyers into bidding more and more. Stick to your guns, remain in charge of yourself and don't be bullied into making bids that you don't want to make. Sometimes if the bids are going in $10,000 lots and you say '$5000', the auctioneer may say, 'Sorry, I'm only taking $10,000 bids' in which case you can reply with a friendly smile, 'That's fine I'm only bidding in $5000 bids – take it or leave it.'

The estate agent is someone else who may apply pressure to keep you bidding if the room goes quiet. S/he will usually stand by your side and say things like, 'I think you're almost there, just another $5000 should clinch it.' Just remember they're all working for the seller so don't be pushed into bidding when you don't want to.

If the bidding doesn't reach the reserve the auctioneer will ask for a few minutes for the agent to consult the seller for updated instructions and if nothing changes will say, 'The bidding hasn't reached the reserve and therefore the highest bidder has the opportunity to negotiate with the seller.' Often they will then go into a back room with the seller and discuss the sale from there. This is what happened with my fourth property.

If the bidding does reach the reserve the auctioneer often announces 'the property has reached the reserve and my instructions are to sell the property this evening' which means that the highest bidder will automatically buy the property, there are no other conditions or reserves to meet. This is when any dummy bidders drop out because if no one bids above them they will be stranded, having to purchase the property.

Auction Tips

Know what the property is worth beforehand

- Know what the property is worth beforehand and don't – under any circumstances – pay more than your pre-determined figure.
- Have approval for finance prior to the auction and don't go above what you can afford/ borrow. It's too late once the hammer has fallen.
- Consider bidding strongly from the start – knock out the competition by standing strong and counter bidding immediately.

Or,

- Consider staying silent right till the end and then coming in with one very strong bid that knocks them for six – my favourite!

Consider one very strong bid that knocks them all for six

Advantages:

- All the action takes place at the one time so you are not left playing games. You can see the other interested parties for yourself.
- If you are confident in auctions and the other buyers are not it can work to your advantage as they may not participate even if they can afford to do so.
- If there isn't much competition due to other auctions being on the same night, or buyers' other commitments, then you may well be up for a bargain.

Disadvantages:

- The thrill and excitement of the auction can lead to other buyers paying more for the property than they intended. That may boost the price beyond your intentions and wastes some of the time you have spent researching it if they out bid you.

- Because you cannot bid 'subject to valuation and inspection' you have to pay in advance for inspections even if you are not the successful bidder.

Private Treaty

Not all properties go to auction; plenty go for sale by private treaty which means that they are advertised for a certain price and then buyers are welcome to make offers at any time.

Why do people prefer selling their properties by private treaty rather than by auction? Well, just as some buyers are afraid of auctions, so too are some sellers as it creates uncertainty at a time when they need stability. They might not like the idea of hordes of people going through their home at an open house and may prefer the agent to show them round individually.

Advantages:

- Sellers who often don't like paying real estate agent fees may try and sell their house themselves. With less experience there may be a greater chance of picking up a bargain.

- Because there is no set selling date, it may be a slower process for the seller to find a buyer. The longer it takes to sell a property, the greater the chance of the seller taking a lower offer.

- It's sometimes easier to understand what you can afford to buy if it has a set price on it. It saves you wasting time looking at ones that are out of your price range.

- If the seller is prepared to accept a lower price than you are prepared to bid, you've just found a bargain.

Disadvantages:

- Sales by private treaty start at a higher price and are then negotiated downwards if there is a lack of demand. This may create a higher price than auctions which start low and build higher if the demand is greater.

- With a private treaty you may have to play drawn-out negotiating games with the agent and other buyers. If you are in a rush to buy you may end up paying more rather than staying silent and waiting for the other party to return your calls.

Summary

There are opportunities to find a good property both at auction and at private treaty sales. The more you understand about both methods of buying, the more you are likely to find what you really want.

The majority of people looking for property are looking for their main home. If you, as an investor, are armed with more knowledge, you should be able to outperform your competition. The more knowledge you have, the better property you should be buying in a better performing suburb.

ACTION PLAN

Attend at least three single sale auctions and three multiple auctions and observe the different styles of bidding. Take notes about what people say, when they bid, and see if you can spot the professional buyers/agents that bid. What do they do that's different?

chapter fifteen

Property Number Three

B y 1999 I had been in Australia for over a year and it was definitely where I wanted to settle. It was also the first time I had rented from someone else. I wasn't happy sharing with so many people while still having the residual feeling of living out of a backpack. Our landlord had been so tight that he had refused to pay for a television aerial so we ended having to split that cost between ourselves. That really annoyed me as I believe a television aerial should be standard to all apartments – his attitude was the final straw that made me think, 'It's time to buy my own place again.'

So – just like my first UK property could be refinanced for the Porsche – I refinanced again to get the deposit for my Australian property.

Exercising the Body and the Mind

Property investing is great for saving on gym fees, especially when you haven't got a car and you're researching hilly beachside suburbs. Sydney's eastern suburbs are particularly hilly. I became quite fit going around and looking at properties every Saturday morning! I'd go viewing all these open houses and I'd be running down one street then up another hill to reach the next one. Up and down all the time, so I bought a secondhand bike. It didn't help me get *up* the hills but it certainly made it easier rolling down the other side! Everyone else was elegantly dressed turning up at these $300,000–$400,000 properties in their nice cars whereas I'd arrive in shorts and T-shirt on a bicycle, sweating. I could see them thinking, 'What's this backpacker doing here? Surely he can't afford to live here!'

> *$300,000–$400,000 sounds so cheap for a two-bed unit compared to the $600,000–$700,000 that you need to spend now*

It's funny looking back – even 4–5 years later $300,000–$400,000 sounds so cheap for a two-bed unit compared to the $600,000–$700,000 that you need to spend on an equivalent one now. I keep saying to myself, 'If only I had bought a few more, I would have made a fortune!' Many of our parents look back at what they could have bought in the 60s and 70s and voice those same sentiments, and the majority of us will continue saying it until we retire, still having done nothing!

I probably saw 70–80 properties – until I eventually saw one that I thought was perfect, well at least it was on the inside. I remember seeing the flyer the week before, but as I was pushed for time I didn't bother going inside as it had a horrible plain brick exterior and the magazine pictures certainly didn't do it any justice. Lucky for me I did make the effort the week after. It had the potential to be a real winner.

Buying a Property in 30 Seconds

It was a two-bedroom unit, on top of a hill in Coogee, NSW, with all bedrooms and the lounge room facing north. Direct sunlight came in virtually all day long so I knew it would be nice and warm, even in winter. Even though it's not right on the ocean it's got sea views from each room. Coming from the UK pretty much all the Poms want sunshine and beach views so if I could get a bed built high enough, I could lie in bed in the mornings and watch the sun rise over the ocean – what more could a guy like me want?

From all the others I had seen I knew it was worth around $400,000 which was the limit of my budget. I wandered up to the agent and asked, 'What's the price range on this one?' to which he replied 'Indications on this so far have been around the $300,000 mark. What are your thoughts?' I had trouble holding back my grin – $300,000 for this, you've got to be joking, it's the bargain of the week! 'I'm not too sure,' I said, playing dumb, 'I've only just started looking' and I walked off into the bedroom. I knew the agent would be under-pricing it to attract more people to the auction, but even so it would be unlikely to climb all the way to $400,000.

I carried on looking round the unit for the next 15 minutes to check that I hadn't missed anything obvious. You can spend weeks looking for a bargain and then when it hits you, you get worried that you might be making the wrong decision, because it seems too good to be true!

From checking out the 70–80 properties beforehand and following up the actual sales prices after auction I had built up a profile of what the agents were quoting me which I could then compare with how much the properties were actually selling for. At the time I found that if an agent quoted say $300,000 for a property then it would roughly sell 10% or maybe 15% higher. Not all properties fell exactly within that profile but 80% of them did. Based on this I thought that even at $350,000 I would be happy to buy it as it would still be $50,000 less than what I had seen other similar ones sell for.

I'd never been a bidder at an auction before, but I had been part of the audience when I was tracking other properties. I was terrified of bidding, it was just like the fear of public speaking. I felt that so many people were staring at me, and even though I had checked everything thoroughly, I was full of self-doubt, and still kept asking myself, 'Am I doing the right thing?'

There was only about a week to go until the auction date and I figured there were a few things for me to do in preparation for the big moment:

- I had already been approved for a mortgage which would allow me to buy a $400,000 property, which I now had to double check with the bank.

- I needed to ring the estate agent to get a copy of the contract for my solicitor to read and advise me.

- I asked the agent to give me permission to contact the strata agent so that I could inspect the strata records to see if the building was insured and historically in good repair. After I inspected the books I then paid a professional to go through the detail as I realised I didn't really know what I was doing.

There were 20 properties listed and 300–400 people in the room. When the property that interested me was announced, rather than fuelling the energy in the room, I kept quiet waiting to see what would happen next. I didn't say a thing. I've never been in an atmosphere like this, it was so electric. The whole crowd really got it. In one particular instance I could see a husband and wife and their kids had set their hearts on a certain property. The same could be said for a rival couple, and I watched as the two families contested this place. People get so carried away you've got to set your limits before you walk in the door, which to me was $400,000. 'If I buy it under $400,000 I'm happy,' was what I had decided beforehand and I would have kept going within that limit. In all that excitement, I consciously tried not to allow my emotions to over-ride my logic.

By the time it hit $355,000 I still hadn't said a word. It was down to the last few dollars when the auctioneer said, 'Unfortunately $355,000 is under the reserve so we're going to move on to the next property….'

Although I was shaking I jumped to my feet and shouted out, '360!' There was dead silence. My two friends who had accompanied me for moral support went bright red as they were sitting next to the idiot who had jumped up at the last minute. The pressure was pumping, I was absolutely shaky, it was so much money.

'Any more takers?' the auctioneer asked the silent room. 'Once twice three times, it's gone. Sold to the man over here.' So from, 'No more bids' I literally got the property 30 seconds later.

I was then ushered into the back room to sign the contract and I was still shaky. It was a weird feeling. My friends remained in the main room as they refused to be associated with someone who so obviously stood out in public, but they were thinking, 'How did that happen? What's going on? What did you do?' They hadn't been involved in an auction before either. I was over the moon once I'd done the paperwork, I walked back into the auction room, grabbed my friends and then went straight to a bar where we ordered the best champagne. Drinks were on me that night, auctions certainly do give a helluva buzz.

Analysis of Purchase

- Viewing 70–80 properties increases your chances of finding the property that is just right for you and below the price you are willing to pay.

- Refinancing a property in the UK released some equity for a deposit and costs of the new property. As I had used 100% bank funds, this was a property purchase where none of my money was used.

Changes I would make with hindsight:

- Even though I knew the right price for the property (based on seeing 70–80 comparisons) I should have still used an independent valuer as a second opinion. It's a small price to pay.

- I should have got a building and pest inspection just in case something was wrong. How is an accountant from the UK going to recognise pest damage? I should have done this, even though the property seemed in good enough shape.

Flat-sharing

I bought this one to live in though I still rented out a room to help pay the mortgage. A lot of people I have come across refuse to share a flat once they hit their late 20s to 30s but just as I did it with my first three-bedder in the UK, I would rather be able to afford bigger investments that will help me retire in my mid 30s than live alone and have to work until I am 65.

Sharing a flat is not much of a hardship to me compared to the benefits. I prefer sharing and I've often had flatmates who rent from me for 3–4 month periods, before moving into their own property. It is a good way of meeting new circles of friends.

All in all this was a great investment. It has grown from $360,000 to $675,000 in under five years. A profit of $60,000+ per year.

chapter sixteen

Use Real Estate Agents to Your Advantage

How to get the most out of a real estate agent

Who Says an Estate Agent Can't Be Your Best Friend?

If you're buying property, real estate agents can be good business contacts, they can give you a lot of information and help – just remain aware that they're working on behalf of the seller. The vendor is paying the agent to sell the property for the best price so agents do everything they can to keep you interested and to get the price up.

Salespeople in general don't always have the best reputation, but try to look at it from their perspective. A lot of people think that secondhand car salespeople are dodgy but imagine being in their shoes – how fed up would you be if you had hordes of tyre-kickers that go out for test drives then never return calls?

Agents will often give you a reasonable amount of information, and you can also draw them out more. As you get to know them they may become more frank with you. They're trying to sell a product, and you're welcome to ask any questions you want. If they don't want to answer your questions they don't have to, but if you're not going to buy it until you know those answers, then they'll need to tell you.

As in any relationship, always try to be friendly and smiley and there's no reason why they won't give you the answers you require.

You never know where these kinds of conversations may lead, but you are sure to pick up a few clues that you can use in negotiations. Answers to questions like these are sure to be useful:

'How much do you think they'd take?'

The answer to, 'How much do you think they'd take?' will give you a good ballpark figure prior to making an offer. It will also give you plenty to think about. It might also uncover whether they're a new salesman, especially if they blurt out something like 'the sellers are absolutely desperate as they've bought elsewhere and will take any offer'.

What makes you think it's worth that price?'

If the agent says, 'We think it's worth $600,000 because we've compared it with other properties that have been sold in the area', reply by asking, 'Which other properties?' They might say, 'We've compared it to these three down the street.' If you've seen those properties, that suddenly gives you a negotiating tool and you'll have something to discuss. You might say, 'They were better properties, they were bigger and had better views, so I don't think this one is actually worth $600,000.' Once they realise you have done some homework they may then quietly reply that, yes, the owners have overvalued it so maybe it is only worth $575,000. Suddenly you've got the agent on your side and admitting that it's worth a lower offer.

'Why are the owners selling?'

Another question you could ask is, 'Why are the owners selling? Are they in any hurry or are they happy to wait until they get their price?' Sometimes people will sell at a cheaper price for the convenience of not moving out. They may be trying to sell early to make certain they sell before going overseas in six months time, while you may not be in a rush to move in. Under such circumstances you might say, 'I'm happy to pay the $500,000 but if they want to carry on living in the property, I'll pay $480,000 or $490,000 but I'll let them stay in the property rent- free for the next six months'. This is possibly a benefit to both of you – you pay less money, while they save in not having to find a place to rent while they're still in the country with all their furniture in storage. Another scenario is that one party may be coming from Queensland and looking to buy in Sydney, while you may be doing it the other way around – moving from Sydney to Queensland. A situation like this offers a lot of common ground, in fact they could be interested in buying/renting your property. Whatever way it goes, they would probably find it easier to deal with you than with someone else.

'How long has it been on the market?'

Another question to ask is, 'How long has it been on the market?' If your prime concern is to get a property very cheaply, this may not be the property for you because you may not be able to negotiate much if it's just been listed. Alternatively if it has been on the market for a while you may have some negotiating room if you offer a quick settlement.

'Have they had any other offers?'

You can always try, 'Have they had any other offers?' The agent may not answer that question. It all depends on how you frame the question and how keen they are to sell the property. If they don't want to answer, they won't. A lot of agents say to me, 'You go round looking at properties, so rather than me tell you, why don't you tell me?' and so they can always push it back.

'How much will it rent for?'

Always get independent checks on specific data about the property

Always get independent checks on specific data about the property but it's still worth asking the question as you can see if the agent knows what s/he's talking about. If the agent is saying, 'A two-bedroom unit in this block was rented for $450 a month ago', go and see a couple of other agents and say, 'I'm interested in buying a property in this particular block. If I bought it how much would you rent it for?' And, if you're buying a property based on a certain rental coming in, remember your agent will portray this figure in the best possible light, so check all documentation. Some friends of mine were quoted $430 a week rent but when they bought the property they only got $400 per week. Unfortunately they had based all their property value calculations on $430 pw rather than $400 – which is not $30 a week they're missing out on but potentially $30,000 they may have overpaid! In those days investment properties were getting 5% rent returns which meant that you would normally pay $400,000 for a unit which rents at $400/wk and $430,000 for a unit that rents at $430 a week. Luckily for them the property market moved up and their unit is probably worth $470,000 just over a year later so they've still made money, which is good.

It's hard to prove whether an agent made a mistake or actually lied to you. I'd say a lot of agents wouldn't blatantly lie but they might try and bend things. So you could ask to see a copy of the lease, which would be a good thing to do. However, the tenant could be a mate of the owner who has agreed to artificially inflate the rent, so rather than relying on what the current tenant is paying check with another agent to see what they could actually rent it for.

Quite often they may say things like, 'It's currently renting for $400/wk but they haven't had a rent increase for the last five years, so we expect it to rent at $430/wk.' There might be some sense in that, if the agent can prove it. If in doubt check everything, it's well worth it.

Keep the Agent Informed

If you're interested in a property make sure you tell the agent because someone else may come in after you and clinch the deal with a higher offer. Unless you were in the loop you would have no way of knowing about it. Being unaware that you're a serious buyer the agent may not bother to call you.

You may have been prepared to pay a better price. So you might have been waiting two weeks for the auction without knowing it has already been sold. Had you made yourself known, the agent would almost certainly have called you to say, 'We've got an offer of $500,000, unless there's a better offer we're going to sell it at that price before the auction.'

Rental Agents

Agents not only help investors buy properties, they also help in getting tenants and managing properties on an ongoing basis. Whenever I need to get new tenants I hire the agent to do all the advertising and the associated paperwork. Depending on where the property is located sometimes I manage it myself, other times I get the agent to manage it month by month.

I manage the majority of my own rentals. My properties are generally well maintained and nothing really goes wrong with them so all the agent really does is collect the rent and pass it on to me. That's why I don't use them as an ongoing managing agent – what's the point in paying them 5%–10% of my rental income per month to do nothing? My rent gets paid into my account by direct debit. All I need to do is double-check that the rent's gone in each month.

If your properties are well maintained and you get on with the tenants, I recommend that you consider managing them yourself. If you get good people in who can afford the rent and pay automatically then there's no hassle. I tell my tenants, 'If you've got any problems just send me an email, but if there's any repairs or anything like that just ring my tradesman and he'll arrange to do all the work.' I then find a good all-round tradesman and leave instructions that if my tenants ring with any problems and the bill is under $250 just go and do it and send me the bill. If it's over $250 then give me a quick call first. The key to this is finding good tradespeople whom you can trust.

Once you start building up a number of properties you need to treat them like a business

When I bought my first two properties I couldn't afford to work this way as every cent counted. I would try to do a lot of the basic work myself. However once you start building up a number of properties you need to treat them like a business. Is it really worth my time trying to save $50 to fix a broken toilet rather than get in a professional? No, because every time I try and fix something I normally end up causing another $100 of damage and still have to get a professional in a few weeks later.

Sometimes I think it's worth using a managing agent, sometimes not. I've got a property up in Queensland (property no. 5) that I get the local agent to manage. It was a brand new property and nothing has really gone wrong with it but I didn't really understand the local market and for $100/mth in agent's fees I thought, 'It's not worth me dealing with it.'

If you've got a lot of properties and you really don't want the phone calls – perhaps you've got a full-time job or you don't want the hassle – under such circumstances it's probably worth commissioning an agent. Sometimes people say it's better to keep a distance from your tenants – especially if they're not paying the rent on time – it's easier for the agent to keep hassling them each week and they will have a lot of processes to make sure they pay on time.

Summary

The better you get on with the agents, the more likely you are to get the inside stories on new properties that are coming on the market and what properties are really likely to sell for.

You need to find an efficient agent to get you good tenants but it may not be necessary to get them to manage the property on an ongoing basis if the property is well kept and unlikely to cause the tenants any problems.

ACTION PLAN

Get friendly with all the agents you meet and see what extra information they can tell you about the property and the seller.

If you meet a good agent and you are considering buying an investment, ask if they have a good rentals department too. Just because you buy a property through one agent it doesn't mean that you also have to rent it out from them.

chapter seventeen
Property Number Four

J ust like I got bored a year after buying my first property, which led me to buy the second, I had a similar feeling after buying the third. And what do I do when I get bored? I go shopping for new toys or new properties.

Again I went shopping along the beaches between Coogee and Bondi, where my thoughts were, 'People always want to live by a beach, they always want to see the sea so I believe it's a good area in which to buy.' I bought my fourth in 2001, again after seeing another 60–70 properties.

I was waiting for the agent to turn up to a viewing when I saw an Auction sign outside the next-door neighbour's house. I liked the look of the place and gave the agent a call. The agent told me it was due for auction within a couple of days, so I would have to move quickly and she seemed happy to show me around the following day. I only got to see the place once but I thought it was unique. Part of the property was on top of a disused garden shed and part was actually on stilts. The current owner had bought the air space and the garden shed from the strata so there was a chance to develop it from a two-bedroom into a three-bedroom unit. I think a lot of people missed that point or didn't necessarily value it. The agent was talking around the $400,000s while I was considering its potential and thinking, 'Taking the possibility of that extra room into consideration and given it is over 100m², it could easily be worth up to $500,000!'

I said that I was interested and requested that she send a contract directly to my solicitor. I had been pre-approved for finance again so I was all set to go.

I was working in an interim management group at Deloitte Touche Tohmatsu at the time. The auction was being held at an hour which clashed with my work. I was supposed to be running a seminar for 100 finance directors and I couldn't get out of it, I was the only person who knew all the guests and I had to introduce them to each other as well give them a market update.

I was driving, mobile on hands-free, listening to Barry making the bids

I was keen on this place but this was one night I couldn't attend the auction. So I gave a $50,000 cheque to my girlfriend Bina and told her to 'hold it', and I asked my flatmate Barry to go and bid for me. I instructed him to bid up to $500,000 while Bina held the 10% deposit. Barry was bidding at the auction, Bina was getting nervous holding the cheque and I was driving from the city to Double Bay with the mobile on hands-free listening to Barry making the bids. Given the circumstances, it was really quite relaxing because it all happened so quickly. I pulled up outside and ran into the auction room precisely when Barry had the bid in his hand at $410,000. Within seconds it was all over, the property had failed to reach the reserve and was handed in. At least it gave us all time to calm down and for me to ask Barry and Bina what had happened leading up to the bids.

When properties don't reach the reserve it normally means that the highest bidder gets the first chance to negotiate with the vendor. The agent takes you into a back room and tries to push the money up by literally persuading you to bid against yourself. Meanwhile they also work on the seller to try and knock the price down and come to some agreement in between.

I refused to bid against myself and said the property obviously wasn't worth any more than $410,000, 'that's all I am paying'. If they wanted to push me any higher, I wanted a get-out clause to make sure I'd made the right decision. In the end I went to $420,000 as a final offer. They still didn't take it and I said, 'I'm not that confident on the construction, I haven't had any time to get my building inspections done and I'm not sure if it's going to fall down. I'll give you $430,000 subject to bank valuation, building inspection and the rest of it, or we can sign the contract here and now for $420,000 and your clients will have a sale. Alternatively they will have to go through another marketing campaign which will take them at least another two months.'

And as a negotiation tool that worked fairly well, because I said, 'It's *worth* $420,000. If you want more money you can have it, but at a cost to you, you're on the line as well.' Then it became their choice. I didn't say, 'I'll only pay you $420,000, take it or leave it' because they may have got stubborn and said, 'We'd rather put it back on the market.' I said, 'Okay, I'll go up another $10,000 subject to everything else.' Anyway, I knew I could always come back afterwards and bid for it again if I was dead keen.

> *Give people choices in sales negotiation.*

I had learned to give people choices in sales negotiation. It then looks as if they are making the decision not you. By offering another $10,000 but having a cost to them attached they could make a decision as to how badly they wanted the extra money. Was it worth having the uncertainty of risking the sale falling over? It just so happened that the seller had already bought another home and was due to settle and the current property needed to be sold in haste. So they took the $420,000 and I was happy because I was prepared to go to $500,000 at a pinch.

Analysis of sale

- You never know when you're going to find the right property, you've just got to keep your eyes open and be ready to act quickly when you do see it.

> *By buying unique properties you are more likely to find tenants*

- By buying unique properties you are more likely to find tenants and be able to re-sell it in the future if necessary. This was a very large unit, close to the beach, with the option to convert it into a three-bedder or a two-bedder + granny flat.

- I bought the property for $80,000, or almost 20% less than I had valued it at, after seeing 60–70 direct comparisons. It's a numbers game, the more you see the more likely you are to find a bargain.

Changes I would make with hindsight:

- I struggled for time to get it independently valued. Now that I have a better relationship with my valuer I am sure I could even persuade him to come out at midnight if I really needed the help.

- The building did need some cosmetic repairs which have been done a year or so later at a cost of about $5000 per unit. I should have also got a building inspection done but as the property is now worth about $675,000 it is no longer significant.

I spent ages trying to get the body corporate to approve my plans for the third bedroom. The strata agents we were using were absolutely useless and so the owners got together and sacked them. We hired new agents and they now manage the property so much better. I have received my development application back from council and am ready to commence building work. I estimate the work should cost about $50,000 and should add $100,000+ to the value depending on the state of the market. The property rose from $420,000 to $675,000 in three years which represents an average growth per year of $75,000.

chapter eighteen

Step Eight: Build a Professional Team

Leverage your time by delegating to experts

A lot of wealthy people may appear to take risks but generally they've thoroughly researched their actions and their advisers have identified all the potential downsides. Whether they're buying properties or building businesses the most successful people in the world work with a team of great professional advisers. They are not necessarily experts at anything specific but they are very good at managing other people's talents. And you can do the same.

> *By delegating my tasks, not only can I make more money, I can also give myself more time*

I make all the major decisions, but by delegating my tasks, not only can I make more money, I can also give myself more time to do the things I need to do, as well as always having a first-class job done by experts. Delegation still involves controlling the main issues, while not having to be physically present 80 per cent of the time, which gives me my lifestyle balance.

Trusted Professional Advice

I started this process of delegation using a broker to get me a loan. I soon learned to delegate everything I could to my team of accountants, solicitors, valuers, building inspectors and tradespeople.

Says John Symond of Aussie Home Loans, 'There are hundreds of home loans, all with varying interest rates, fees, charges and other variables that could well cost home buyers a lot of money. The best policy is to get *trusted professional advice* on how to navigate your way through this very complicated space.' The same can be said for the way all your professional advisers handle their area of specialisation on your behalf.

So every time I go into an auction I get my solicitor to check all the paperwork, I get a valuation, and I get it pre-approved for finance through my mortgage broker.

Accountants

Even though I am a qualified accountant, my time is better spent looking at deals where I can make tens of thousands of dollars year-on-year rather than saving a couple of hundred dollars here and there on individual transactions. By hiring an accountant who specialises in property accounts s/he is more likely to be right up-to-date with what I can claim and what I can't.

Making the decision to delegate is one thing, the other is ensuring that you delegate to the right type of person. I recently changed accountants and described what my plans were to someone to whom I was referred. His advice was to pay off all my debt. I was then referred to another accountant who specialised in looking after clients who are into property investing. In fact, he was a property investor himself and he answered my question by saying, 'I had twice as much debt as you at your age, and if you take on good debt for investing in property, I believe you should carry on. I would also suggest buying under a company and trust structure which will be more tax effective.' Guess which accountant I chose!

> *Your strategy should be robust enough to get you through*

According to Ron Switzer of CPA Australia, 'You want to have a situation where you have a long-term relationship with your accountant or financial planner. Normally there would be formal reviews of your portfolio twice a year (which can be more often now with technology). You do this to maintain an up-to-date analysis of how you're tracking. If something untoward happens, your strategy should be robust enough to get you through. When things go awry, people often need some guidance and counselling to get them through these sorts of circumstances. This is one of the advantages of working with an accountant.'

Conveyancers and Solicitors

Conveyancers deal with the transfer of property whereas solicitors will deal with a whole range of other legal matters.

Sometimes conveyancers are cheaper because they're doing a systematic job, which may be all that is required in a straightforward property purchase. Balance this saving against the advantages of using a solicitor who can look at the total picture to see if there are any other issues. I generally go through a solicitor in preference to a conveyancer but either/or is fine.

Some people choose to buy a Do-It-Yourself conveyancing kit which saves them a few hundred dollars on hiring a professional. Why do it yourself? The amount of money they're risking by doing it themselves is unbelievable. They could potentially wipe out their whole portfolio if they make a mistake on a half a million dollar property.

Just pay your solicitor and get the job done properly.

Even though I always use a good solicitor I certainly read/browse through my contracts because I like to get an understanding of them.

You've got to make sure you're doing your homework; you can't just rely on other people. You've got to back up your information. If something still goes wrong at least if I've used a solicitor then I'd be able to use their insurance to remedy any problems.

> *There's no way the average person can read a 50-page legal document*

Never sign anything until your solicitor has seen it. There's no way the average person can read a 50-page legal document on the spot and understand what it's saying. Why would you put your name on a $500,000 document that you haven't read? It could be saying anything. A lot of people assume that just because it's a legal document it's going to give them protection, but if you haven't written it, don't sign it. Contracts are like mortgage documents – no one ever reads them, they just sign. And customers assume that because it's a nice big bank they're going to do the right thing. I send it all to my solicitor, 'Here's the contract, check it out' and he'll come back with any points of concern.

I don't have the legal know-how to understand the finer points of a contract and for the sake of paying $700–$800 for a professional job it's not worth my time doing an unprofessional job. I'd rather be finding another property where I can make $50,000 or $100,000.

Superficially most property contracts are pretty similar, the difference is usually in the Special Conditions that are at the back. You've definitely got to read these because they are specific to your particular purchase.

Valuer

Get an independent valuation on any property you are serious about purchasing so that you know whether or not it is a fair price. If you're only going to learn one thing from my book make it, 'always get a valuation'. They can range from $200–$500 depending on how much time and detail you require. Even though the banks will order one when you apply for a mortgage it is too late to benefit you as you may have already bought the property at auction. Your inability to get finance because you have paid too much doesn't mean that you can back out of the contract.

> *If you're only going to learn one thing from my book make it, 'always get a valuation'*

You can find national firms under Valuers (Real Estate) in the Yellow Pages or on the Internet. When you are choosing a valuer ask, 'What kind of experience have you had in these locations?' So I wouldn't send my eastern suburbs valuer up to Queensland, I'd get a local Queenslander for that job. But if it's around the local Sydney area, he's great.

Before making a bid, I don't always check 70–80 properties any more. If I know a good property is available, I'll send in my valuer before doing anything else, and if he confirms it's a good deal then I'll go and look at it myself. This is especially useful when buying interstate because it saves me so much time.

If you're going to get it done, you might as well get it done properly. I get my valuer to produce a 20–30 page report on a specific property which includes about 12 comparisons and usually costs me around $440, whereas for $200-$300 a bank valuer only comes up with a two-page report with maybe only two to three comparisons. It's worth paying the extra money to know your valuer has been inside and has checked it out properly, whereas if I paid half the amount s/he'd only have time to sight the property and take a rough guess.

I may still bid above the valuation at auction as sometimes they are conservative, but if I'm bidding more than 5%–10% above the estimate, I would know that I'm moving into riskier territory.

Strata Searches

When you buy into a block of units, you get a 'Strata Title' because you all own the block together, and you all get a vote in the running of the property. The strata will have records to show that the building is insured and it will also confirm what fees you'll have to pay to the strata each month. You need to know 'everything', for example, the roof could be in disrepair, and the strata may have agreed that all owners must come up with $10,000 each to pay for a new roof before the end of the year. If you were to buy that unit you'd get a nasty surprise in six months' time if you hadn't checked the strata.

In the description of my third property purchase I checked the strata records for the unit block I was looking at buying. I then realised that it was better to get a professional to check over the records because – as they were doing it all day every day – they would have a better understanding of what insurances and other legalities should be in place. They may also have a better understanding of expenses that may be incurred in the future. These services cost $100–$200 and can sometimes be provided by your valuer as part of the valuation.

If you've checked the strata books you may be able to use that information in your negotiations: 'The property's worth $500,000 but I've got to pay $10,000 in six months' time, therefore I'm only willing to pay $490,000.'

Building Inspector

It's also important to get a building inspection. The building inspector will look at the structure of the building to see if it has any problems like rising damp, concrete cancer or anything structural that may cost you money over the coming years.

If you get a building inspection done and the building falls down you should have some recourse. Use certified building inspectors who have insurance, so that you can pursue them if something does go wrong.

Sometimes you need three separate people for (1) a valuation, (2) a strata search and (3) a building inspection. However, there are companies that handle all three. I've had all three done through a valuer, other times I've used three separate sources.

Tradespeople

Because of the amount of work I've put into property in the past, and the fact that I use other people's skills, I now probably spend less than one hour a month on my existing properties. For example, my first St Albans property – I get an email once or twice a year about a maintenance issue.

A lot of people use distance as an excuse for not buying property but when you've got a good tradesperson that no longer applies.

> *It's not worth getting out of bed for $50*

Because I'm running my own business, it's not worth my time to fix smoke alarms and broken toilets myself. I prefer to pay tradespeople, but when I started off I couldn't afford to do that. I couldn't afford $50, that's how tight my money was – whereas now I realise it's not worth getting out of bed for $50 which is why I tell the tradespeople that if it's under £250 don't call me, just do it.

Times change. The first property you buy is always the hardest – you might have limited funds and you're probably not sure what you are doing. As time goes on it gets easier and the bills get less and less significant.

Buying the second property is a bit easier, and properties 5–6 are so much easier that even bills like $5000–$10,000 are not a big hassle because the renovations are adding to the price of your property. If your property is increasing $50,000 a year surely you must realise that once in a while it needs a bit of TLC to keep it going.

Other Services

And then I got to thinking about lots of other services that can be inexpensively bought. It went further than buying property, it was also about living in that property, especially living with your flatmates and having to clean up after them. I didn't want to be their servant. And that's the way I've always lived.

Cleaners

When I bought my first house I rented a room each to two friends who were slobs, and I thought, 'There's no way that I'm going to work all day and study all night to come home and clean the toilets and wash the bath out for these guys!' So we paid a cleaner $25 for three hours cleaning a week and each of us contributed $8 for never having to clean the house. For $8 – the price of two beers – why would you waste your precious weekends cleaning ?

Ironing and car wash services

Why spend hours ironing your shirts and washing your car when for something like $25 someone else could do it? I'd rather enjoy my free time.

Internet shopping

Why spend hours around the shops on a Saturday buying toilet paper and the rest of the things that you use week in and week out? Just get it all delivered and spend your time shopping for more exciting things. I don't want my wife or my girlfriend doing it either.

For $7 why not use the Internet shopping facilities on your computer? Some people spend all Saturday at the shops – which is half their weekend gone. I think, 'Why would I want to spend time doing that kind of rubbish when I could spend the whole of my spare time down on the beach or on the boat?'

I'm just waiting for the fridge that knows I'm out of milk, yoghurt and cheese, and orders it in automatically.

The best four tips when investing in property, are according to Bernard Salt, Property Partner, KPMG Chartered Accountants:

1. **Read widely and often.** Make it part of your regime.

2. **Access primary reports** and familiarise yourself with the data, e.g. values, population, planning reports.

3. **Appreciate that the world changes over time.** The world as we know it now will shift before the end of the decade. What is impossible now, may be possible then.

4. **Never accept advice from one source.** Check it from several angles. Experts often have a point to prove! Have faith in your own gut feeling.

Summary

Delegating your work and leveraging your money are two of the big keys in property investing

Delegating your work and leveraging your money are two of the big keys in property investing. Leveraging your money makes it go further and delegating your work gives you more time to do the more enjoyable things in life, whatever they might be.

If you're going to delegate you need to have a professional team around you that you can trust to do a good job. It takes time to find people for your team and often asking other property investors is the best way to go.

I always ask my advisers to see if they invest in property themselves because if they 'walk the talk' they are more likely to have a better knowledge on the reality of the decisions we're about to be making.

Don't negotiate too hard on their fees as they may not be able to afford to give you the service that you really need. I recommend my accountant to all my investing friends but I still don't know what he charges per hour – his advice is worth whatever bill he sends me (only to a point though, Mario!).

ACTION PLAN

Go and 'interview' your team. Get referrals from friends, colleagues and other property investors. Ask them why you should hire them and what can they do for you.

chapter nineteen

Property Number Five

My fifth property is an example of how to buy a property without spending your own money.

Three years ago my flatmate introduced me to a friend who'd read in the London *Financial Times* that Australia was the place to invest. He proposed putting $300,000 cash into Australian property which he knew nothing about and his problem was that he would have to rely on an unknown estate agent to select one for him, which is generally a high risk. So I suggested to him that if he bought a $300,000 property on spec he probably wouldn't be buying a good one and he may get something like 3%–4% rent return and perhaps a 5–10% capital gain. He would certainly make money but it would require a lot of effort and there would be associated risks.

I suggested to him that if he put up the $300,000 I would take it to the bank and get a mortgage on the strength of that deposit. I would then borrow maybe $700,000 – and so instead of him buying a $300,000 property with no mortgage, we would buy $1 million worth of property with a mortgage. We'd be buying two or three properties with that million dollars which would generate more rent than one $300,000 property. And because we'd buy in better areas the properties would be going up more in value.

I said that I would give him 7% return on his money out of the profits, so straight away he would effectively get double his return on his $300,000 that was earning 3% sitting in the bank. Say for instance property went up by 10%, he may get $30,000 profit on his $300,000, but the $1 million holdings would go up by $100,000.

If I then paid him 7% on his money that would be $21,000 which would leave us another $80,000 profit, which if we split 50/50 would give him $40,000.

If he invested by himself he would get:

- $9000 in rent based on a 3% return

- $15,000–$30,000 capital gain based on 5–10% growth

- He would have to go through the hassle of buying from 12,000 miles away and take on the risk associated with that.

If he invested with me he would get:

- $21,000 in rent based on me paying him the 7% mortgage rate on his money

- $40,000 capital gain based on 10% growth on $1m less the $21,000 interest on his money which gets taken out first

- I would do all the buying, negotiation and management and because my only profit is in the capital gain then I am motivted to buy as best I can

- He is then secured by a second mortgage over the properties and a charge over my company.

You might then say 'Well what about the cost of the mortgage?'

$1m property at 4% rent	$40,000
$750,000 mortgage at ($1m + 5% costs – $300,000 deposit)	($52,500)
Yearly loss	($12,500)

After depreciation and a tax rebate on any loss the loss is only a matter of a few thousand dollars at most which will be split 50/50.

In summary:

I calculated a way to double the return on his money

- I calculated a way to double the return on his money.

- I've also given him $40,000 worth of capital gain whereas before he was only getting $30,000.

- Also because I'm managing the lot, he doesn't have to do any work.

- Because he would be investing with no local knowledge it is unlikely that he would be as good at picking growth suburbs and so the capital gain percentage on my properties was likely to be higher than his.

After a bit of negotiation he was happy with this deal and so we started the ball rolling by buying one property in Algester, Queensland.

Land	$117,000
Construction	$157,000
Costs	$9000
Total Paid	$283,000
Mortgage	($216,000)
Deposit needed	$67,000

He put in $75,000 which was the deposit and we got a mortgage and stamp duty from a bank. The rest of his money went into the costs for solicitors and we put $8000 in the bank to cover any losses if the rent didn't meet the mortgage. We got $280 a week rent and the mortgage cost us $1400 a month, so we lose $200 a month on it but the value of the property went up $60,000 in the first year from $280,000 to something like $340,000 which was very good. His proportion of the return was about $33,000 while mine was about $27,000 so he's already made 50% return on his money. Even if the property stopped growing, on average over five years he's already got 10%–15% compared to his 3% in the bank

Cash buffer $75,000–$67,000 =	$8000
Rent $280pw x 4.3 =	$1200
Mortgage $216,000 x 7.7%	–$1400
Loss per month before depreciation	$200

> *I've bought half an interest in a property and it hasn't cost me a cent*

The benefit to him is he's got more return for no work or effort – the benefit to me is I've bought half an interest in a property and it hasn't cost me a cent because he's fronted up all the money. I mention this because anyone can do deals like this too, once you are knowledgeable. Obviously when you are starting out it's hard to get the credibility but when you tell people that you will use their solicitor, you will get an independent valuation and will also give them some security, what have they really got to lose?

> *A deal like that is really satisfying because both people gain*

It takes a bit of working out to understand exactly how this all goes together but there's benefits to both sides by pooling the resources – he had the money but he didn't have the time, the skill or the location to take action. I have the knowledge, the skill and the time to put it together but I didn't have the money, so it's a 50/50 partnership with both people putting in different things. Just like when I did the deal for my second property with my father – I had the skill, the knowledge and I selected the actual property which made good money for both of us, whereas he had the ability to get a mortgage which I didn't have. So both of us were effectively putting in 50% and we've made over $200,000 each. He wouldn't have been motivated without me and I couldn't have done it without him. A deal like that is really satisfying because both people gain, but the skill is to actually cut that deal.

You may have friends who work 60 hours a week or a family member who doesn't have the time or knowledge to invest in property – but they've got the money and the income to get a mortgage. So anyone who has the time can say, 'I'll find the property, I'll spend weeks and weeks of research at the weekend, I'll make sure that we're buying it under value (or at a decent value), I'll look after all the tenants, I'll look after all the hassles, I'll look after all the maintenance, but you come up with the deposit, we'll take the risk 50/50 and we'll split the profits 50/50.' The other party wouldn't take action without your help and you can't do anything if you haven't got the money, whereas together you can create a good team.

Summary

Foreign investors can normally only buy brand new properties in Australia and have to be approved by FIRB, the Foreign Investment Review Board.

Buying a house and land package in Algester, Queensland was a really good growth investment, especially as I got a joint venture partner to pay all of the costs and deposits. We previously spent about 12 months trying to negotiate on buying secondhand properties in NSW but they all fell over.

I was overseas when the property got built six months later but as my solicitor had come from a property development background, he was able to make the final inspection for me. The building company handed the keys to a local estate agent who within a few weeks got me a tenant paying 5% rent.

Changes I would make in hindsight

None. I must be getting better at organising my professional team!

chapter twenty

Step Nine: Start with a Lower Offer

Understanding offers will save you money

Many of us are happy to haggle in a market stall or have no worries about knocking a car salesman's price down – but how many of us really seek bargains when it comes to real estate?

People sell for a whole horde of reasons and their thoughts and confidence will also peak and trough through the sales cycle. If you made 10 offers $50,000 lower than you thought they were really worth on 10 different properties, is there a slim chance that one may be accepted? I should think the answer would be yes.

You say, 'Would the sellers take an offer?' Certainly the agent can say, 'We priced it at $600,000 and we're sticking to it' or 'We're going to auction', but most agents will always take an offer. If you put an offer to an estate agent by law they have to take it to the seller.

Things are different from state to state and the law is constantly changing. Get your solicitor to double-check everything before you make any offers or commitments.

It's well worth making some low offers

It's well worth making some low offers just to get into the practice of how things work. You've got nothing to lose by doing so and if your offer is serious there's always a longshot chance it's going to be accepted, especially when the property market is down or if there is pressure on the vendor to sell.

Whatever the real estate agent, the auctioneer or anyone else says, whether it's up for auction or for sale, you can make any offer you want at any point of time. And you can offer any figure. So, if a property is up for $500,000 and you come up with something ridiculously low like 'I'll offer $300,000', the agent may say, 'That's a stupid offer, the seller's not going to accept it', by law that offer has still got to be taken to the seller. If you feel the agent isn't doing this, you can make direct contact and say, 'I'm willing to offer this price for your property and I don't believe your agent told you that.' It's certainly not going to help your relationship with the agent, but if you want to buy a property and you think you can negotiate better with the seller direct, there's nothing to stop you doing so.

Until I am absolutely ready to make an offer, I never tell the agent exactly how much I am prepared to pay for any property. Nor would I say how much I've got in my budget, because if they have an offer on the table for $500,000 but they know potentially I can pay more, they'll try to push me to my limit, and they'll do the same to you. Those kinds of figures you'd generally want to keep to yourself.

If you want to exert even more pressure attach your 10% deposit

---

If you're making a low offer and you want to ensure that the real estate agent takes it to the seller I suggest giving a formal and specific instruction like, 'I want to offer this amount and I want you to take it to the seller.' If you want to make it even stronger, put it in writing, and if you want to exert even more pressure attach your 10% deposit. In this instance you could say, 'I'm offering $300,000 – here's a cheque for $30,000 to cover the 10% deposit and my offer is subject to…' (whatever you want to make it subject to). You can have it subject to valuation, finance, building inspection or whatever else.

Make Offers to Private Sellers

There's a limit to how much money you can save, but there's no limit on how much money you can make. Some people are so tight when it comes to real estate that while they're saving on one hand they're throwing even more money away on the other.

Estate agents may charge 2%–3% commission – which on a $500,000 property can be $10,000–$15,000. Some vendors want to save that money by doing it themselves. I believe an agent always generates more interest than people who sell their own properties, agents get things moving because they speak to so many potential buyers. They also negotiate every day of their lives.

If I see someone advertising their property for sale themselves I think there is always ample opportunity for a good negotiation on price.

Making an Offer

If you're serious about a property:

Make yourself known. Tell the agents enough about yourself so that they take you seriously.

Build credibility. To build their confidence, tell them you've been conditionally approved for a loan. Telling them makes them realise you've done your homework beforehand and you're not wasting their time. Describe the kind of properties that you have already looked at and mention that you have made offers in the past (but don't mention how much was in your budget).

Broach the subject. Tell them you're interested in making an offer on the property.

State the figure. Confidently state the figure you wish to offer.

Leave a 'get-out' clause. Add words that express that this offer is subject to your solicitor's approval of contract, possibly finance, valuation and building inspection, all of which still leaves you with a get-out clause if you need one.

Summary

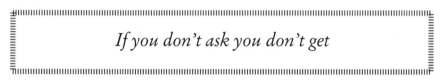

If you don't ask you don't get

An old boss told me if you don't ask you don't get – if you don't ask for a pay rise you won't get one. The same goes for property. If you don't make an offer, you're not going to pick up a bargain.

ACTION LIST

Find 10 properties that you are interested in buying and have a good idea of what they are worth. After checking with your solicitor consider making an offer, subject to valuation/finance, 10%–20% below what you think it is worth.

If you get no joy find another 10, as you might not be succes

chapter twenty-one
Property Number Six

Once you have a few properties you can diversify your portfolio by purchasing different types of properties in different types of location. You could try something different and it's a wonderful feeling if it really takes off. As each property is only a small proportion of your overall holdings, any risk you take by moving into unfamiliar territory shouldn't have drastic financial consequences.

The company that I trusted to look after my mortgage affairs also had a sister company that dealt with new property sales and in particular ones that were being sold off-the-plan. I'd never heard of 'off-the-plan' before I came to Australia. The director of the company was on a similar wavelength to me and we often discussed property issues.

He described how the developer needs to pre-sell 50%–60% of a block of units before the bank will lend the money to start construction. Because the block of units won't be completed for another – say – two years you can buy 'off-the-plan' today for $450,000 but when it's actually built it may be worth $500,000. The idea is that the developer sells at a discount because the buyers are taking the risk of not actually seeing what they are buying. Furthermore, the market should, hopefully, rise over that two-year period which makes the property even more valuable than the fixed price of $450,000.

The second advantage is that you don't have to spend the whole $450,000 all at once – you would normally only put down a 10% deposit for the same growth. Therefore, on the $450,000 example (worth $500,000 when built) the $45,000 deposit will have generated $50,000 in equity by the time the construction is complete. And you'll have just doubled your money.

Off-the-Plan

So I checked out an off-the-plan property in Hornsby, Sydney because I wanted to diversify geographically and I wanted to own a completely different type of property. The building itself was six stories high and my unit was on the fourth floor. It was an 80-square metre two-bedroom unit which also had a 60-square metre balcony which was a sizeable outdoor area, all facing north-east. Because the property hadn't been built, rather than have an open inspection I reviewed the plans around the boardroom table and had to visualise what it would look like. The next day I went to the empty site to see how the construction would fit into the local surroundings.

I then got an independent valuation because I didn't know the Hornsby area. My valuer compared it to 12 different properties, some secondhand, some brand new and some not yet constructed. I agreed to buy the unit at the asking price of $450,000 which was my valuer's price. I knew that he was likely to be conservative so I was happy to proceed.

Rather than putting down a 10% deposit and having my money sit in someone else's bank account, my broker suggested that I get a deposit bond or a bank guarantee. These are basically guarantees or insurance policies that promise to pay the developer the 10% deposit when the building has been completed. The deposit bond companies will generally only give you a deposit bond if you have equity in another property that can be used as security. They ask you to prove that you have sufficient equity (normally two to three times the amount of the deposit needed) but they don't actually secure it with a second mortgage. Alternatively they want to see that you have it in savings and have been approved for finance for the rest of the loan.

I bought a deposit bond for $45,000 which cost me about $2500 based on the $150,000–$200,000 equity I had in property No 3 in Coogee.

I've come across a number of investment companies or 'clubs' which sell over-priced properties to mums and dads who are buying their first investment property. However, this company seemed legit. So many people do so much due diligence and checking of prices when it comes to their own house and then they do absolutely no research when it comes to an investment. They just accept the price they are told.

> *Labelling it an 'investment' doesn't save it from being a bad property*

Labelling it an 'investment' doesn't save it from being a bad property. They may tell you they're selling a $500,000 property at the wholesale price of $465,000 but why would any money-making operation sell it for less than it's worth?

One of the things I like about buying secondhand property is that it's all sorted in one transaction. You can buy it today, at today's price, you can get a mortgage today and hopefully you'll get a tenant today. You're not waiting for construction to take place.

Off-the-plan properties can be advantageous because you pay today's price at a later date and hopefully get to own it when it is worth a much higher price. The disadvantage is that you don't know whether it will definitely go up and you may have trouble raising $450,000 finance if the property has slumped to $400,000.

Rent Guarantees

Many investors are initially concerned about having tenants as they need the rent to pay off their mortgage. To make a sale more attractive, a lot of investment companies offer rent guarantees. A rental guarantee can be seen to have all the answers but often they've increased the price of the property to artificially inflate the rent. A property is not worth more because the rent is artificially inflated.

Here're the numbers – say the property is worth $450,000, the investment group might pitch for $500,000 with a rent guarantee of $500 per week (instead of $400, which is its real value). That probably sounds appealing, i.e. a $500,000 property with a $500 pw rent guarantee rather than the real figure of $450,000 with a $400 pw rent. However, the investment group is propping up the rent by $100pw which, over 12 months, costs them only $5000. However, if they've added $50,000 to the price of the property, the investment company has made $45,000 out of it!

Then at the end of that two-year stint it's back to reality – you're probably only going to get its real value, the $400 per week which it should have been all along.

Summary

> *Using deposit bonds means that you get the benefit of the ongoing capital gain without having to buy the property up-front. I bought a $450,000 unit for $2500.*

Buying properties off the plan by using deposit bonds means that you get the benefit of the ongoing capital gain without having to buy the property up-front.

I bought a $450,000 unit for $2500 with an expected completion date of 18 months.

Changes I would make with hindsight

I think I did it right this time. My solicitor checked over the contract and my valuer did a full valuation. I could do no other inspections as construction hadn't yet started.

SECTION D

KEEP GOING!

chapter twenty-two
Step Ten: Never Sell

How to realise your profits without selling your properties

S o many people think that you have to sell a property to realise the profit that you have made on it but that's certainly not the case.

Say you bought a property for $300,000 and it went up to $400,000 and you are considering selling it to buy a bigger property:

- The agent would charge you 2%–3%
- Then you may have to pay the new 2.25% sales tax (in some states)
- Then you might have to pay 25%–50% capital gains tax
- And then when you buy the next property you are going to have to pay 5% in stamp duty and legals, etc.

How much would be left of your $100,000 profit after paying off all those taxes and expenses and how much hassle is it all going to be?

If it generally costs 5% of the property value ($20,000) to sell and another 5% to re-buy another property ($20,000) and you pay say 25% in capital gains tax ($15,000) you would be losing roughly half of your profit. As an alternative let's look at refinancing.

Refinancing

Why pay high costs and taxes in selling a property

Why pay high costs and taxes in selling a property when you can easily refinance for a fraction of the cost and with a lot less hassle? If you always refinance rather than sell and rebuy, it makes it even more important to choose the right property in the first place as you may then own it for the next 30–40 years.

Having decided to refinance you can go to your bank and say, 'My property used to be worth $300,000 – now it is worth $400,000. I would like to borrow against the $100,000 that it has gone up by and want to use those funds to put as a deposit on another investment property.' If you sell your property and the bank would be happy to lend you money on a new one, then why wouldn't they just as easily lend on the new value of your existing one? They do.

The bank can then set you up with a 'second mortgage' account and lend you – say – 80% of the $100,000 increase which is $80,000. By refinancing you are effectively doing the same thing as selling a property and buying it back the next day minus all the transaction fees and the tax. The cost of this should be under $1000.

Before refinancing	2000	2004
Property value	$300,000	$400,000
Mortgage	−$240,000	−$240,000
Equity	$60,000	$160,000
After refinancing		
Property value		$400,000
Mortgage 1		−$240,000
Mortgage 2		−$80,000
Equity		$80,000

You can then go to the bank and say, 'I have $80,000 from refinancing my current property and I now want to buy another $300,000 property and I want an 80% loan.' Depending on your serviceability the bank will then lend you $300,000 x 80% = $240,000 and ask you for $60,000 deposit which you'll take from the $80,000 you've just refinanced, leaving you $20,000 for costs and stamp duty.

> *You've got to be able to withstand the fluctuations*

To banks, serviceability is a big issue, because they lend on cashflow as well as equity.

Says Ron Switzer of CPA Australia: 'You've got to be able to withstand the fluctuations and you need predictable cashflows in any form of investment. However, there may be unpredictable cashflows or indeed other demands on your cash that have nothing to do with investments.' So create a buffer zone that enables you to always meet your mortgage repayments.

New property value	$300,000
5% costs	$15,000
Buffer zone	$5000
Total needed	$320,000
80% mortgage	$240,000
Cash from refinancing	$80,000
Total	$320,000

When you refinance you can generally use the funds for any purpose – such as paying off credit cards, renovating your property or for buying another one. If you spend it on luxuries just remember you have *not* got rid of your debt. It is still there against your house and it is almost definitely not tax deductible.

Your bank or mortgage broker should be able to explain in more detail what is involved as you can have various options of split loans, offset accounts, lines of credit, etc., which make it easier to distinguish what money is for investment purposes and which is personal.

Unless you've got a high income it can get pretty hard to borrow money for 3–4 properties. Sure, property assets can get you out of the workforce but quite often you'll need to work to keep the banks convinced that you can afford those mortgages. Even if you're making money from the properties, the banks are very conservative and might say, 'We'll only take into account 75% of your rental income because you may strike a period of vacancy.'

Refinancing and Buying a Porsche

When I bought my first property at 22, I knew nothing about refinancing. One day I saw a bank ad which was about releasing the equity in your home for home improvements or for buying a car. I had equity in my home, but although I wasn't interested in home improvements I was certainly interested in buying a Porsche. I never thought I would have enough money for a car like that but this advertisement planted a seed in my mind.

I could have a Porsche at the age of 24 for only $50 a month

The minimum amount I could refinance was $35,000 and it so happened that $30,000 was a nice price for a 10-year-old Porsche. So I refinanced my first property and I bought a bright red Porsche. The loan repayment on the mortgage would only go up about $150 a month over 25 years, so I thought, 'I could have a Porsche at the age of 24 for only $150 a month', effectively costing me very little to drive the car I fancied at the time.

Refinancing for personal expenses is not a good thing from the perspective of taking out 25-year loans to pay for luxuries you don't really need.

However I believe in living for today as you don't know what's going to happen tomorrow. By that stage I had bought a property for $50,000 under value and the property had continued to rise by another $50,000. Having made $100,000, I thought, 'Why not take 35% of that out and have some fun?'

That property has risen from $200,000 to $750,000, a profit of $550,000. Spending $35,000 of that on the luxury of a Porsche is less than 10%, which I believe is conservative. I might have had trouble justifying spending $500,000 of it on a Lamborghini! Keep it in perspective.

For those of you that are not into material things, you might have other interests – travel, renovations, or anything you like. Mine is a passion for speed and world class machinery, which made the Porsche a dream come true.

Owning that car was one of the best memories of my early life. After picking it up I turned up at my parents' house in the evening and said, 'I've got a new car, come and see it.' I was grateful that Dad didn't ask how I raised the money, so I never needed to explain how the profit on the house bought me the car. After saying goodnight to my parents, I drove it all night.

That was possibly the biggest thing that clicked in – and why I am in property: because it makes money. That's when I started learning. It made me realise that if a house goes up in value you don't have to sell it to take out the profit. That increase in property value gives you a choice of how you spend your money, your life and whom you want to share it with. Friends around me had not bought property for fear of being tied to a mortgage, but to me it gave freedom and the chance to do things I could not previously afford to do.

Summary

If it costs you 5% to buy a property and 5% to sell it, why not just refinance it and buy more property with the increase in equity? Part of that equity can be used for the odd luxury but beware of increasing your debt if you're not also increasing the amount you're investing.

ACTION PLAN

Speak to your bank or mortgage broker about how much equity you have for potentially investing in other properties. Just because it's there, you don't have to use it all. If you set up the facility it will cost you very little and will give you a source of emergency funds or a buffer zone to pay for unexpected emergencies.

chapter twenty-three

Buy Property without Using Your Own Money

How to make your money go further

An infinite return on your money is possible if you manage to buy property without using any of your own money

An infinite return on your money is possible if you manage to buy property without using any of your own money. Typically this happens when you borrow 100% from the bank. Often the bank will only lend you 80%, so it's a case of finding the other 20% from another source. The more innovative you get, the more property you can buy.

The idea behind the following suggestions is basically to propose a method of buying property with no money down or with limited money down.

Says Ron Switzer, CPA Australia, 'It's my accounting background emerging here but I have seen some experiences where investments have been over-ambitious. Usually it's in the property development area, as opposed to the rental market, which can be lower risk. On the other hand, you take that risk – recognising that the bigger the risk, the bigger the potential reward. However, you need to remember that the converse may also occur. If you are more averse to risk, you can for example buy a smaller residential property that's going to have a certain market yield at the time. You also make a judgement for the longer term based on the geographical area in which you are purchasing the property, as well as other factors.'

Joint Ventures

A joint venture is a deal where two or more parties, both with different resources, come together to buy a property. The reason they do a joint venture is because they couldn't achieve the same results without the resources/talents of the other party. A typical example of this is where a high income earner has the finances but doesn't have the time or knowledge whereas his/her counterpart has the time and knowledge but no available funds. By working together they can create a mutual profit.

Knowledge is an important negotiating tool. It enables you to approach people, who aren't sure what to do with their money, with a suggestion that is as sound as the property market. If you are prepared to do the legwork, trace the progress of real estate, follow the press ads, ride your bicycle from property to property on a Saturday morning to the point where you are 'in the know', you will certainly accumulate valuable information. You will *know* where to buy, and you will also spot the prices that are inflated.

My first 'joint venture' was property No. 2 which I bought with my father, although I didn't understand the terminology at the time. Even though I put some money into the deposit, the majority of it was borrowed. Most people don't like to approach family for assistance when buying a property, but if you take it to them as a business deal rather than asking for a handout, you are more likely to succeed.

My fifth property (Queensland) was a joint venture with Paul from the UK who had the money to invest but didn't have the local knowledge nor the physical ability to buy. Even though I had the money to buy it myself, half a house for no money down is a better return than a whole house on a $75,000 deposit. I didn't have any special inroads. Paul just happened to be a friend of a friend, and he was looking for an investment property in a country where he had no expertise. As with my father, Paul's joint venture with me was extremely profitable for both parties. I am now looking at doing other joint ventures on a grander scale to build my property portfolio up much more quickly than if I did it by myself.

There can be downsides to having joint venture partners, especially when involving family. If two people are involved in the decision process and those people's goals change over time it could ultimately lead to conflict. Therefore each party needs proper legal protection so that they are not merely acting in good faith, but are covered in the event of things falling apart, either on the personal or business level:

> *Always use a solicitor and get the agreement legally documented*

No matter which side of the equation you are on, keep everything above board:

- Always use a solicitor and get the agreement legally documented
- Decide the course of action to take in advance if the worst situation should occur. For example, if we fall apart Paul and I have agreed that the property will be sold by our solicitor after seven years, and the profits divided as agreed from the outset
- Clearly set out what each party is bringing to the deal and their respective responsibilities
- If you are putting money/equity into the deal, ensure this is for a fixed amount. Be extremely cautious if you are putting your family home on the line
- No matter if you are responsible for the selection, or the other party is making the purchase on your behalf, always get an independent

valuation on the property, so that you have a professional opinion – for your own protection.

The Guarantor

The risk to the parents is minimal

According to Anthony Bell, Bell Partners, 'There's a couple of different ways of getting your deposit, one of the ways is getting parents to help. That doesn't mean the parents actually pay any cash. It's not, "Dad give me $50,000", there's usually a second security, a security over their parents' place – that gets you in. Then you renegotiate two years down the track when the equity in the property has grown and the bank hands back the deeds to the parents' house. The risk to the parents is minimal. The risk to the parents is if the property selected was over-purchased leading to a forced sale.'

Off-the-plan

If the property market is moving up and is likely to do so for the following few years, off-the-plan properties can be good ways of enjoying the capital growth of the property without having to completely finance it at the time of purchase. Often you can buy property at today's prices with a 10% holding deposit and not have to settle for another two to four years. These days with the creation of deposit bonds and bank guarantees, rather than put up a 10% cash deposit you can offer up the equity in your other properties instead at a cost of a few thousand dollars.

When it comes time to settle and the property has risen significantly in value it may actually self-finance if the bank values it at that future price rather than the price actually paid.

For example, if you bought a $400,000 property in 2001 and the bank would only give you an 80% mortgage at the time, you would have been required to put $80,000 down as a deposit. However, if you had bought that property off-the-plan using the equity in your own home as security for a deposit bond then it would have only cost you $2000–$3000. If, for instance, it was time to settle in 2004 during which time this property had appreciated to $500,000, and the bank were prepared to give an 80% mortgage on its current value, then it would be giving you a $400,000 mortgage on a property that had only cost you $400,000 – making it 100% finance.

	Buy Now 2001	Off-the-plan 2004
Property value	$400,000	$500,000
Mortgage 80%	–$320,000	–$400,000
Equity	$80,000	$100,000
Purchase price	$400,000	$400,000
Mortgage (above)	–$320,000	–$400,000
Deposit needed	$80,000	0

Conversely instead of settling in 2004 you could sell the now-completed property instead, in this way turning your $2000–$3000 deposit bond into a $100,000 profit which is 30–50 times return on your money.

Vendor Finance

Vendor finance is another way of negotiating a purchase if you are limited by not having a deposit. Say you want to buy a property for $300,000 and you are entitled to the First Home Owners Grant which would pay your costs, and you also fell into the stamp duty-free threshold, all you would lack would be the deposit. Depending on your income you may need somewhere between 5% and 10% deposit, let's say 10% or $30,000.

How long would it take you to save $30,000?

How long would it take you to save $30,000? Maybe three years, by which time that particular property may have risen to $390,000 based on 10% growth – so saving for a deposit in a growing market clearly puts you further and further behind. Let's say that you managed to find a seller who'd had trouble selling a property and was now open to taking an offer.

What if you said, 'As you haven't been able to sell your property I will offer you $300,000 if you will lend me the 10% deposit I need to satisfy the bank. Instead of you putting that $30,000 in the bank and earning 3%, I will repay you that money at 7%. I will pay you the interest monthly and within two years the property should have risen in value enough that the bank will let me refinance and I can then pay you back your $30,000 in full. I will get a solicitor to draw up a straightforward agreement that says that I will give you security over your old property so that I cannot re-sell it without paying you back first.'

Not everyone is going to go for this deal but if you keep asking there is surely a chance that one will? If they are not in a hurry to spend the money immediately, why wouldn't they lend you 10% of the property value at double the rate they would get from the bank? Especially if they originally bought the property for $150,000 – they are only playing with extra profit – and if no one else has offered them the $300,000 that they hoped for, their only other alternative would be to drop the price.

Would this work well if your parents were thinking of downsizing? You would have bought a property for no money down

Would this work well if your parents were thinking of downsizing and you were keen to buy the family home?

And as far as you are concerned, you would have bought a property for no money down.

Beyond the Square

The examples above are not simple concepts if you've not heard of them before, but with the right professional advice they are reasonably straightforward to arrange. If you educate yourself in this way there is no reason why you can't think beyond the square, come up with new ideas and generate property agreements that are profitable to everyone who deals with you.

These joint venture ideas all came out of reading books and attending conferences. While all my friends were spending their weekends in the sun on the beach, I was going to seminars about property.

> *The money I can earn for others in the long term is 10–20 times what they could earn for themselves by leaving it in a savings account*

If you want more, get out of your comfort zone and try a bit more. The money I can earn for others in the long term is 10–20 times what they could earn for themselves by leaving it in a savings account. So I'm now trying to create win-win deals with other partners. Maybe you've got an idea that would work well with me? Why not give me a call?

Even if I only take a 10% profit of their portfolio gain, we can all earn more money than if they – or I – did it alone. By taking a percentage rather than a fee, I am more incentivised to get them properties that really do grow in value.

John Edwards of Residex, describes himself as 'more of a financial engineer than anything else'. Residex was formed to gather information on the future of lending and to allow institutions to invest with good knowledge of the market. He says, 'I realised that future generations weren't going to be able to afford housing, and we had to come up with a method of doing that.

'Housing basically has a cashflow that is unique to itself. It has in

Australia high levels of capital growth and rental return, and that's really a consequence of a shortage of land and the maturing of the cities and while you're in the change-over period from being a country where there's plenty of land and low population to cities where there's plenty of land still, but not enough money to be able to afford the development of infrastructure, you get this high rate of capital growth and low rental return.

'Ultimately it will change over, we'll go back to having lower rates of capital growth and higher levels of rent, but for the next generation or so we're looking at low rate, high capital growth.'

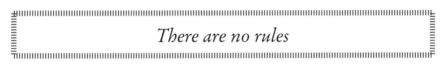

There are no rules

Summary

There are no rules. No matter what you start with, you can create something fantastic. Knowledge and money is the key and you need to find a way to get either one or the other, or ultimately both.

Work on your strengths and invest some time and money into building knowledge. Each day you spend learning is still a day spent not earning, so if you can find people to help fast track you, it may cost you some money in the short term but will enable you to grow wealthier in the long term.

ACTION PLAN

Analyse your financial situation and assess your limiting factors, i.e. time, knowledge, money.

Start networking to see who can help you with what you are missing. Ask your advisers, speak to your family and read books and home buying magazines. Do anything that will help you create ideas to buy property without spending your own money.

I'm always open to new ideas.

chapter twenty-four

Your Own Real Estate Portfolio

The purpose of this book has been to show you how your lifestyle dreams can become a reality through investing in property and to get you out of the workforce. We're all time poor and so I've tried to narrow my strategy down to 10 easy steps that are quick to read and to put into action.

If you really want more out of life, visualise your ultimate dream and write it down *now*.

Step One: Set your goals

> *If money were no object, what would you be doing?*

Wealth isn't about money, it's about choice. You've got to choose what you want to do. What is your ultimate goal?

The big picture is that if money were no object, what would you be doing? How would you be living your life? There is no reason why this should be denied. You can stop work, own 10 properties if you plan it and logically work through your finances as I have explained in the preceding chapters. You can have anything you want if you do something about it now, otherwise you will find yourself continually turning up at the office, working 9–5, and still be no closer to buying your first property.

Step Two: Figure out what you own and what you owe

Running multi-million dollar personal finances starts by finding what finances you've got today.

What have you got and what do you need? If you can organise what you've got now, you've got a better chance of taking action when you've got some serious money.

Write down your own personal balance sheet, work out those assets and liabilities, get a clear picture of the balance sheet that you really want and understand it well, so that when the time comes to face the financial people they will know that they are dealing with someone who knows what they are talking about.

Step Three: Face your bank, or your broker

Having worked out what you want, both ultimately and in the immediate future, and how you stand financially, puts you in a confident frame of mind when the time comes to approach a lender. Whether you decide to approach a bank or a broker is up to you – each has particular advantages which may suit your personal situation. But walk in confidently knowing that if you have done your homework, you are a suitable person to whom they can lend money, because they can see that you have the income, the discipline and the resources to pay it all back on time and as agreed.

Doing this gives them confidence in you when the time comes for them to extend your loan so you can buy future properties, which you are sure to do if you follow this way of multiplying your property portfolio.

Step Four: Research the suburbs

If Australia continues to grow at 10% on average, that means that some suburbs will grow by 20% while others won't grow at all. Make sure that you are investing in the ones that are maximising the money you have tied up. And you can only do this by doing your own research because no one looks after your money as well as you do.

I wore out a lot of shoes learning about investment properties in the localities that interested me, and I did not wholly trust the agents who had their own vested interests (and those of the sellers) at heart. However, I learned how to use them to my advantage and I suggest you do the same.

I now consider them to be my friends.

Step Five: Look for these things in a property

I want properties that are going to grow in value because that's what creates wealth

First and foremost, I want properties that are going to grow in value because that's what creates wealth. Secondly I want properties that are going to be easy to rent because that's what pays my mortgage.

If I can add value to the properties by doing minor renovations, that will increase the growth even if the market isn't moving. Buying unique properties in good locations ensures that I always get a tenant, and I get a high valuation, making it easier to buy further properties.

Step Six: Get a valuation

Buying an over-priced property is the best way to lose your wealth, buying an under-priced property is the best way to increase your wealth.

No matter how much I have researched a property, in the end I always turn to a professional valuer to confirm its true value. Having an independent valuation is the sure-fire way of ensuring a novice doesn't get ripped off buying an overpriced property.

This is my No. 1 tip.

Step Seven: Get comfortable at auctions and private treaties

Remember the Golden Rule: S/he who has the gold makes the rules. So if you've got your finances in place, you are in the power seat and there is no reason to be shy, not at auctions, not when entering private treaties, not anywhere. However, it does help if you familiarise yourself with the buying environment, the rituals, the procedures and the lingo.

Show up a few times, get confident, and after a while you will quite naturally find yourself holding up your paddle and making a bid. Stick to your budget. Good luck!

Step Eight: Build a professional team

Property investors don't have to be experts in all areas

Every professional has an area of first-class expertise, all of which is available to you at a price. Property investors don't have to be experts in all areas, and when you consider the amount of money at stake both in terms of what you are putting on the line and the profit you stand to make, frankly $200–$700 is neither here nor there.

But if you make a mistake, you're risking possibly $300,000 – maybe $1 million. I don't think it's worth the risk. I always use professionals and I recommend you do too. You won't regret it.

Step Nine: Start with a low offer

Start with a low offer – they can only say no.

And sooner or later you might get a big surprise. Someone might say yes, and you will find yourself thousands of dollars in front! Like so many things, it's a numbers game.

Step Ten: Never sell

> *If you've bought well in the first place why sell it?*

Out of all the things I have taught people over the years, the one which surprises them most is the realisation that they don't actually have to sell their current property in order to buy more. In fact, buying and selling – or selling and buying – will cost you possibly 10% of the property value, which could be 50% of the money you stand to make. I've never sold and never intend to do so.

I've seen so many people regret selling properties because they could have made so much more if they had held more to them. I now find it a challenge to find someone who is happy that they sold!

If you've bought well in the first place why sell it?

Peaks and Troughs

> *The longer they sit on the fence, the higher the prices rise*

Many people have wanted to buy property but haven't done so; now that they missed the last boom they are afraid they cannot afford to buy where they previously wanted to live. The longer they sit on the fence, the higher the prices rise. If you are one of those people, why not learn from your previous mistake and go and buy somewhere you can afford. You can still rent in your suburb of choice but at least you've got a foot in the door and your property is rising.

If you've made a decision to buy but are waiting for the next boom, consider the 'contrarian' investors who start investing when the market is flat. By buying then, you will enjoy the benefit of the whole property boom. If you wait for the boom to be published in the press, by the time you get in it will almost be over.

Home buyers who keep their homes for 5–10 years wouldn't even notice a major fluctuation when their $600,000 property falls to $550,000 and back up, and to be honest it doesn't really matter too much. If you bought at $600,000 and lost your job, or got divorced and you were forced to immediately sell, then you'd potentially make a loss. But if things keep ticking over and you wait a couple of years, it'll be bounce back to $600,000.

Last Thoughts

If you look though magazines like the *BRW Rich 200* or its equivalent elsewhere in the world, you will note that the biggest fortunes are either made or underpinned by property. The people on the Rich 200 choose to buy real estate because they believe it is a solid investment.

The other characteristic of wealthy people is they take action, and that's exactly what the other people don't do. According to Anthony Bell, Director, Bell Partners, the difference between people who have got wealth and those who haven't is, 'They make positive choices and have the ability to invest in property and never get into a situation where they are forced to sell.'

So whatever you do – even if you're going to make a mistake – do something.

A large part of writing this book, and writing my courses, is because – above all – I want to motivate people to take action.

If you want to build up your property equity so you can restructure your loan and drive a Ferrari, you can. I did!

See you on the track,

Chris Gray

Glossary of Terms

Asset – something that has a monetary value/something that puts money in your pocket

Balance sheet – assets and liabilities – a statement of what you own and what you owe

Credit file – a report that records information when you have applied for credit, the amount and the type. It also lists when you have defaulted on payments.

Joint Venture – an agreement between two people

Liability – something that you owe to another person/something that takes money out of your pocket

Leverage – borrowing money to purchase a higher value property

Mortgage Broker – someone that introduces customers to lenders

Mortgagee – a person who has taken a loan out on a property

Mortgagor – the lender who has given a loan on a property

Net Assets – total assets less total liabilities/net equity/net worth

Vendor – a person that is selling a property

Index

FEAST2FEED

My book is about how wealth can give you freedom and choice in how you run your life. Wealth also gives you the ability to help others. FEAST2FEED is just one of many charitable organizations that I support and I hope you can too."

FEAST2FEED (www.FEAST2FEED.org) is a volunteer network of concerned global citizens committed in the fight to eradicate hunger and ease human suffering. As a charity without borders, political affiliations, or religious basis, we endeavour to raise necessary funds and awareness through community-based programs and initiatives. Uniquely staffed completely by volunteers and existing purely by sponsorships, this grassroots organization mobilizes community aid abroad through an affiliation with the United Nation's Food and Agriculture Organization, (www.fao.org) and its Telefood and Feeding Minds Fighting Hunger programs. By endowing sustainable long-term projects in developing countries, FEAST2FEED with Telefood works towards a planet permanently free from hunger. The FEAST2FEED: Action Aid team work on individual appeals for disaster stricken regions aligning with humanitarian entities with a local presence in those regions. This enables us to provide short-term aid and relief whilst government and international aid agencies are assessing need and assigning surplus.

Become a part of the Internet's most effective volunteer network by joining the Legacy Project at www.FEAST2FEED.org and take an action step.

Chris Gray

Feast2Feed Incorporated
10 Cook Road
Centennial Park, NSW 2021 Australia
+61 2 9380 2490 phone
+61 2 9380 2212 fax

Personal Summary

Make a note of every new idea you pick up and want to put into action

page no.   Comment

....

....

....

....

....

....

....

....

....

....

....

....

....

....

....

....

....

....

page no.	Comment
....	....
....	....
....	....
....	....
....	....
....	....
....	....
....	....
....	....
....	....
....	....
....	....
....	....
....	....
....	....
....	....
....	....
....	....
....	....

page no.	Comment
....	....
....	....
....	....
....	....
....	....
....	....
....	....
....	....
....	....
....	....
....	....
....	....
....	....
....	....
....	....
....	....
....	....
....	....
....	....
....	....

page no.	Comment
....	....
....	....
....	....
....	....
....	....
....	....
....	....
....	....
....	....
....	....
....	....
....	....
....	....
....	....
....	....
....	....
....	....
....	....
....	....

page no.	Comment
....	....
....	....
....	....
....	....
....	....
....	....
....	....
....	....
....	....
....	....
....	....
....	....
....	....
....	....
....	....
....	....
....	....
....	....
....	....
....	....

page no.	Comment
....	....
....	....
....	....
....	....
....	....
....	....
....	....
....	....
....	....
....	....
....	....
....	....
....	....
....	....
....	....
....	....
....	....
....	....
....	....
....	....